THE ARCHIVAL TURN IN FEMINISM

D1560051

THE ARCHIVAL TURN
IN FEMINISM

Outrage in Order

KATE EICHHORN

Temple University Press
PHILADELPHIA

Library
Quest University Canada
3200 University Boulevard
Squamish, BC V8B 0N8

Temple University Press
Philadelphia, Pennsylvania 19122
www.temple.edu/tempress

Copyright © 2013 by Temple University
All rights reserved

Published 2013
Paperback edition published 2014

LIBRARY OF CONGRESS CATALOGING-IN-PUBLICATION DATA

Eichhorn, Kate, 1971–
  The archival turn in feminism : outrage in order / Kate Eichhorn.
  pages cm
  Includes bibliographical references and index.
  ISBN 978-1-4399-0951-5 (cloth : alk. paper)
  ISBN 978-1-4399-0953-9 (e-book)
  1. Feminism—North America—History—20th century. 2. Zines—
Publishing—North America—History—20th century. 3. History—Sources.
I. Title.
HQ1121.E33   2013
305.42097—dc23

2013006604

  ISBN 978-1-4399-0952-2 (paperback: alk. paper)

Printed in the United States of America

082714P

A book in the American Literatures Initiative (ALI), a
collaborative publishing project of NYU Press, Fordham
University Press, Rutgers University Press, Temple University
Press, and the University of Virginia Press. The Initiative is
supported by The Andrew W. Mellon Foundation. For more
information, please visit www.americanliteratures.org.

Contents

Preface   vii

Introduction   1

1   The "Scrap Heap" Reconsidered: Selected Archives of Feminist Archiving   25

2   Archival Regeneration: The Zine Collections at the Sallie Bingham Center   55

3   Redefining a Movement: The Riot Grrrl Collection at Fales Library and Special Collections   85

4   Radical Catalogers and Accidental Archivists: The Barnard Zine Library   123

Conclusion   155

Notes   161

Works Cited   179

Index   185

PREFACE

In the early to mid 1990s, as many established feminist institutions were falling into decline, girls and young women across North America started to plot a new revolution. Armed with little more than scissors, glue, and stolen time on copy machines, they made zines an integral part of their movement. Valuing expediency over posterity, however, their hastily produced publications rarely pointed beyond the moment of production—the temporality of girl zines was the present. By extension, nothing about these publications necessarily pointed to the archive.

Centered around the category of girl, itself temporally bound, rather than the more enduring category of woman, the temporal orientation of zines permeated feminist activism and cultural production in the 1990s—a point emphatically expressed by the title of Bikini Kill's self-produced 1991 cassette release, "Revolution Grrrl Style Now." If a previous generation of feminists had funneled their energy into permanently changing the status of women through the entrenchment of new laws and institutional policies, in the 1990s a younger generation of feminists often appeared to be more interested in the political efficacy of tactics, which are by definition effective only to the extent that they remain fleeting. In this context the annual march and monthly newspaper started to give way to more ephemeral interventions from the flash mob to the zine. Although the performance and affect of an annual protest or flash mob frequently do overlap, just as the content and aesthetic of a monthly newspaper and zine often share more rather than less in common, their promise is different. If the former promises to return until proven irrelevant (as demonstrated through events such as International Women's Day and Take Back the Night marches), the latter makes no such guarantee—its power to bring about change is located in, rather than despite, its unpredictability.

Thus, rather than build institutional bases from which to restructure the social world, feminist activism in the 1990s was about making do in a world where it had grown increasingly difficult to ignore precariousness, even the precarious nature of past political victories. After all, in contrast to a generation of women who came to feminism in the late 1960s to early 1970s, girls and young women in the early 1990s were both the inheritors of a myriad of feminist political gains and institutions and the inheritors of a movement suddenly in decline. Riot Grrrl and, more broadly, third wave feminism appeared just as many second wave feminist institutions, especially those in the culture sector, including feminist presses, publications, record labels, and bookstores, were beginning to come apart, owing to both the internal pressures of volunteer burn-out and infighting and the declining external funding for explicitly feminist endeavors. Being a young feminist in the early 1990s—the era of Susan Faludi's *Backlash* not Robin Morgan's *Sisterhood is Powerful*—meant being always already aware of the fact that political gains, even those that appear most entrenched, can never be taken for granted.

Throughout the 1990s, differing temporal identifications and orientations would also surface as a major source of tension within the feminist movement. The "generational debates" that reached their peak around the turn of the new millennium were often rooted in accusations: older feminists dismissed younger feminists as politically naïve and thereby either unaware of the need for long-term institutional change or oblivious to *their* histories of struggle; younger feminists complained that the so-called "second wavers" were simply "behind the times." This book is *not* an attempt to rehash the generational debates that plagued the feminist movement in the 1990s (these debates have already received adequate attention elsewhere), but I am concerned with what these debates obscured—namely, the extent to which feminists born since the late 1960s were and continue to be invested in both the future and the past, albeit not in a way that easily grafts onto a previous generation's investments in futurity or history.

As explored in detail throughout this book, by 2000, the documentary traces of early to mid 1990s feminisms, including the zines that played an essential role in the spread of Riot Grrrl, had begun to migrate from basements, closets, and filing cabinets to community-based collections and established university archives across North America. As it turned out, despite the seemingly ephemeral nature of Riot Grrrl—a movement defined by an explosive repertoire of gestures, styles, performances, rallying cries, and anonymous confessions reproduced on copy machines—it was also a movement that had been collecting, preserving, and preparing itself for the archive all along. More surprising, when revisiting the documentary traces of 1990s feminism in archives and special collections, it is apparent that, beyond collecting the documentary traces of their own history, younger feminists (some no longer all that young) were also gathering up traces of feminist activism and cultural production from the 1970s and 1980s. To the extent that this is a book about archives, it is also a book about the feminist movement and, more notably, what has become of the movement during the past two decades.

Because this is a book about the feminist movement (specifically, the feminist movement in North American since the 1990s), its timing has ironically been called into question. Some of my closest readers—trusted colleagues and friends who all identify as feminists—have worried that this may not be the "right time" to publish, as they sheepishly put it, "such a feminist book." As we all apparently know, even those of us who are engaged in scholarship and teaching that is labeled "feminist," feminism is neither a great way to market a current book nor a subject upon which one can safely wage a case for tenure. When telling colleagues that I was working on a book about *feminist* archives and special collections, rather than something a bit more seemingly contemporary—let's say, queer archives or activist archives—I admit to feeling at times like a traitor, but to whom or what? To my politics? To my time? As I argue throughout this book, however, it is important to consider the political efficacy of being in time differently, that is, being temporally dispersed across different eras and generations. Indeed, this is precisely why the archival turn in contemporary feminism is as much about shoring up a younger generation's legacy and honoring elders as it is about imagining and working to build possible worlds in the present and for the future.

* * *

Like archives and collections of all kinds, book-length projects, which invariably unfold over several years, collect a myriad of ideas, voices, and perspectives along the way, many unanticipated at the moment of the project's inception. This book is no exception. My earliest articulations of this book proposed to trace the migration of feminist zines into community-based collections and university libraries and archives. Six years later, my focus has both broadened to include feminist documents in general and narrowed to focus more exclusively on university libraries and archives. The change in scope reflects the fact that during the course of researching this book, I learned about other projects focusing specifically on feminist zines, including Alison Piepmeier's *Girl Zines: Making Media, Doing Feminism* (2009) and Janice Radway's ongoing research on the "afterlives" of girl zines, and about the development of collections of related materials, which include but are by no means exclusively focused on zines, such as the Riot Grrrl Collection at Fales Library and Special Collections at New York University (now the focus of chapter 3).

This book has also benefited from the insights, encouragement, and support of many colleagues and interlocutors. For providing funding at the onset of this project, I thank the Faculty of Arts at Ryerson University where I taught from 2003 to 2008. For providing the working conditions that made writing this book possible, I thank my colleagues in the Culture and Media Studies and Gender Studies programs at The New School and extend a special thanks to Dominic Pettman and Ann Snitow. For work space and library access during my first Montreal winter in 2011, I thank Will Straw and the Media@McGill Institute. The prehistory of this book, however, points to another place and time. On this account, I am especially grateful to the intellectually and politically engaged communities of feminist and queer scholars I encountered at Simon Fraser University and York University in the mid 1990s to early 2000s, to the late Barbara Godard for her theorizing on feminist cultural production and for demonstrating what it means to live both for and in archives everyday, and for debates and imaginings carried out under the auspices of the "beyond stasis collective."

Many parts of this book were first delivered as conference papers, and, as a result, parts of this book have benefited from the feedback of audiences encountered at McMaster University's The Archive and Everyday Life Conference, Barnard Center for Research on Women's Activism in the Academy Conference, the 2011 meeting of the Canadian Association for Cultural Studies, the "Office of Recuperative Strategies" at the Pratt Institute, and the Protest on the Page Conference at the University of Wisconsin-Madison. This book has also benefited from the experitise of the editorial teams at Temple University Press and the American Literatures Initiative. Special thanks to Mick Gusinde-Duffy and Janet Francendese for seeing this book through the press at its various stages of production.

This book is most notably indebted to the insights and enthusiasm of several astute readers and reviewers. I am especially grateful to Alison Piepmeier, Ann Cvetkovich, and Janice Radway for their thoughts and support on this project since its inception and to the insights and participation of the librarians and archivists who agreed to collaborate with me along the way, including Lisa Darms, Emily Drabinski, Alana Kumbier, Lisa Sloniowski, Kelly Wooten, and most notably Jenna Freedman, who also connected me to many of the readers and participants listed above.

Finally, I wish to thank my partner Angela Carr whose attentiveness to language, politics, and the beauty of both the material and the abstract is always a source of great pleasure. This book has benefited in innumerable ways from her editorial insight and her mind.

THE ARCHIVAL TURN IN FEMINISM

Introduction

In early 2009, Jenna Freedman, one of the activist librarians I met during the course of researching this book, invited me to attend a conference at Columbia University on the subject of "archiving women."[1] Freedman, the founder of the Barnard Zine Library and a speaker at the conference, used the opportunity to discuss the development of the collection she established in 2003 and to explore some challenges she has since faced while collecting, cataloging, and preserving highly ephemeral, self-published feminist and queer documents for both an open stacks collection and an archive. Regularly asked to deliver talks at academic conferences and activist forums, Freedman spoke as she always does, from her standpoint as a reference librarian and "accidental archivist."[2] Despite the fact that she is well known among feminist and queer librarians, archivists, and academics for founding and overseeing a major collection of contemporary feminist documents and for her related activism and scholarship, Freedman seemed surprisingly out of place at this gathering in the Faculty Room at Columbia University's Low Library. In addition to being the only frontline librarian invited to speak, she was one of the only presenters who also chose to foreground her direct connection to community-based and activist collections. Freedman's seemingly token presence at the conference was especially notable, however, because the event had been promoted as a "conference bringing together scholars and archivists" and exploring questions directly related to activist archiving, including "How have feminist archival practices engendered new historical narratives and new political agents?"

Some participants at the conference shared the perception that the structure of the panels and the prevailing discussions had inadvertently reinforced the idea that archives and special collections exist simply to *serve* scholars' research mandates or to house scholars' own papers but not necessarily to generate and promote the circulation of ideas, cultural interventions, and activism in the present. Following a report about the symposium on her Lower East Side Librarian blog, where Freedman admitted, "I'm not saying that the conveners deliberately dissed practitioners, but I did feel like an afterthought . . . ,"[3] the debate about the conference continued. Kelly Wooten, a collections development librarian at Duke University's David M. Rubenstein Rare Book and Manuscript Library, remarked, "Not that we're the only people qualified to talk about these things, but I think we (women's history archivists) should have been part of the conversation."[4] Emily Drabinski, an instructional librarian at Long Island University and librarian-scholar, agreed, emphasizing that the exclusion of frontline librarians and archivists placed practitioners' contributions to theorizing on the archive under erasure.[5]

Many years after the "archival turn" in the humanities and social sciences has made it commonplace to understand the archive as something that is by no means bound by its traditional definition as a repository for documents,[6] I was surprised to discover that for most of the presenters, "archiving women" appeared to have less to do with women archiving than with women being archived. In other words, the emphasis appeared to be on understanding women as potential subjects rather than as central agents of the archive. As someone who carries out research in and on the subject of archives and special collections, however, the Archiving Women symposium and its fallout also clarified several things I had been observing about feminist archives over the past decade, and these observations form the basis of this book.[7]

For a younger generation of feminists, the archive is not necessarily either a destination or an impenetrable barrier to be breached, but rather a site and practice integral to knowledge making, cultural production, and activism. The archive is where academic and activist work frequently converge. Indeed, the creation of archives has become integral to how knowledges are produced and legitimized and how feminist activists, artists, and scholars make their voices audible. Rather than a destination for knowledges already produced or a place to recover histories and ideas placed under erasure, the making of archives is frequently where knowledge production begins. The archive, however, is also where a younger generation of feminists have most visibly come to terms with their ressentiment toward second wave feminists—an effect of feeling, as Astrid Henry observes, that "the second wave already lived through all the big battles, making us merely the beneficiaries of their efforts."[8] It is where they often appear to be more preoccupied with preserving a previous generation's achievements than running roughshod over their histories of struggle. Throughout this book, I emphasize that archives and archiving hold specific significance for feminists born since the late 1960s because their knowledge and cultural production have become—by necessity—deeply entangled in the archive.

The Archival Turn in Feminism: Outrage in Order explores the centrality of the archive and practices of archiving in the activism, cultural production, and scholarship of feminists born during and after the rise of the second wave feminist movement. While the book builds on other queer and feminist readings of the archive,[9] it is unique in both its specific focus on feminist archives and its emphasis on understanding these spaces as repositories of not only *affect* but also *order*. For this reason, although I pay considerable attention to the history and influence of eclectic community-based collections,[10] the case studies at the center of this book examine three institutionally based archives and special collections: the zine collections housed in the Sallie Bingham Center for Women's History and Culture at Duke University's David M. Rubenstein Rare Book & Manuscript Library; the Riot Grrrl Collection at New York University's Fales Library and Special Collections; and the Barnard Zine Library at the Barnard College Library.[11] Specifically, I examine how these collections, each established by activist archivists and librarians since 2000, *resituate* feminist knowledges and cultural production in ways that directly respond to contemporary internal and external struggles. As this book emphasizes, rather than approach the archive as a site of preservation (a place to house traces of the *past*), feminist scholars, cultural workers, librarians, and archivists born during and after the rise of the second wave feminist movement are seizing the archive as an apparatus to legitimize new forms of knowledge and cultural production in an economically and politically precarious *present*.

Activist Archives in a Neoliberal Era

By now, we can say with some certainty that the archival turn has proven to be a much longer preoccupation than many other recent "turns" in cultural theory. Long after the Foucault effect in the late 1980s to early 1990s, which offered a theoretical basis for rethinking both history and the archive, and the subsequent publication of Jacques Derrida's *Mal d'archive* and *Archive Fever* in 1995, which inspired countless publications, conferences, and debates about archives and archiving across disciplines, the archive continues to attract the attention of scholars, artists, and activists. Variously adopted as a theory, curatorial trope, poetic form, subject of inquiry, and site of research, the archive's appeal shows few signs of waning. But what has been and continues to be the archive's draw as a subject of inquiry, site of research, and critical practice? More important, to what extent might the archival turn be relevant to understanding the contemporary terrain of politics and identity?

Contemporary theorizing on the archive and even much of the recent research carried out in archives suggests that the archival turn has been motivated by anything but a desire to unequivocally recover the past. Derrida's *Archive Fever* is a book about time, memory, and technology but not necessarily a book about history. As historian Carolyn Steedman wryly observes, "In Derrida's description, the *arkhe*—the archive—appears to represent the *now* of whatever kind of power is being exercised, anywhere, in any place or time."[12] Ann Stoler's theorizing on archives is about the "grids of intelligibility" or systems of knowledge that produced particular regimes of truth under colonial rule. In this respect, her turn to the archive is as much a turn to philosophy and, more specifically, epistemology as it is a turn to history. Ann Cvetkovich's theorizing on the archive is first and foremost about trauma and desire and, by extension, survival; moreover, she admits, where the archive is thus deconstructed, the quest for history can at best be understood as "a psychic need."[13] The archive appears in all three of these remarkably different texts not as a place to recover the past but rather as a way to engage with some of the legacies, epistemes, and traumas pressing down on the present. To understand the archive's appeal to cultural theorists, artists, and activists at this particular historical moment, we must first consider what sort of *present* we occupy.

While one might speculate, as I have done elsewhere, that the timing of the archival turn is primarily related to the digital turn (a technological and epistemological shift that brought the concept and experience of archives into our everyday lives[14]), here I suggest that the archival turn in the mid 1990s may also be understood as an effective response to the far-reaching economic and political impacts of another turn—the turn to neoliberalism. Following David Harvey, I maintain that neoliberalism is a theory of political economic practices that propose "human well-being can best be advanced by the maximization of entrepreneurial freedoms within an institutional framework characterized by private property rights, individual liberty, unencumbered markets, and free trade" and which thereby place the state itself in a position where its primary function becomes protecting such assumed freedoms and rights.[15] My argument regarding the archival turn and neoliberalism runs along two lines. First, I maintain that neoliberal restructuring profoundly eroded our sense of political agency, which compelled us to look for new ways of manipulating the present through a turn to the past. Second, I argue that, as neoliberal restructuring rendered anti-economic endeavors increasingly untenable, the archive was adopted as a viable and even necessary means to legitimize forms of knowledge and cultural production in the present. Thus, the turn to neoliberalism and the turn to the archive can be understood as connected along both conceptual and material grounds, and, as I demonstrate in this chapter and throughout this book, this connection may be especially apparent in the context of contemporary feminist scholarship, cultural production, and activism.

Although it is always difficult to attempt to define one's own era from within, it may be at least as difficult to ignore the fact that since the 1980s, our *present* has been deeply and irreparably shaped by neoliberalism. If neoliberalism is difficult to ignore, it is because its reach is irrefutably expansive. Little has been left untouched by neoliberalism, which has not only affected our economic and political conditions and consequently the structure of our everyday lives but has also altered our conceptions and experiences of time, history, and, most critically, social agency. On this basis, however, we can also begin to trace the relationship between the neoliberal and the archival turn. If we have become more interested in the archive both as subject of inquiry and creative locus for activism and art during the past two decades, then such interest is owing in part to the archive's ability to restore to us what is routinely taken away under neoliberalism—not history itself but rather the ability to understand the conditions of our everyday lives longitudinally and, more important, the conviction that we might, once again, be *agents* of change in time and history. Most disturbing about neoliberalism, after all, is not what it makes possible but rather what it apparently makes impossible. As Henry Giroux observes, "Within the discourse of neoliberalism that has taken hold of the public imagination, there is no way of talking about what is fundamental to civic life, critical citizenship, and a substantive democracy. Neoliberalism offers no critical vocabulary for speaking about political or social transformation as a democratic project. Nor is there a language for either the ideal of public commitment or the notion of a social agency capable of challenging the basic assumptions of corporate ideology as well as its social consequences."[16]

As contemporary theorizing on the archive demonstrates, archives do many things, but they do *not* necessarily stage encounters with the past. Following Foucault's premise that the archive not be understood as something that "safeguards" or "preserves" past statements—not be understood as something that "collects the dust of statements that have become inert once more"[17]—contemporary theorizing on the archive has emphasized the archive's status as a historiographic rather than a preservationist technology. Indeed, precisely such a premise prepared us for Derrida's claim that "archivization produces as much as it records the event."[18] Rather than simply reflecting a desire to understand the past, the current archival turn reflects a desire to take control of the present through a reorientation to the past, and in this sense the archival turn under neoliberalism may be understood as a realization of what Wendy Brown describes as "genealogical politics."

Brown summarizes Foucault's reformulation of Nietzsche's genealogy as follows: "Through its inquiry into the 'past of the present,' in which the categories constitutive of the present are themselves rendered historical, genealogy exposes the power of the terms by which we live; it does violence to their ordinary ordering and situation, and hence to their givenness."[19] In other words, genealogy first and foremost defamiliarizes the very assumed order of things. For example, to the extent that categories (for example, identity categories) and conditions (for example, the assumed necessity of a forty-hour work week or the assumed normalcy of the two-parent heterosexual family) become naturalized over time, genealogy reveals that such things are by no means historical norms and thereby not uncontestable features of our everyday lives. In this way, genealogy is not only a historical methodology but also a powerful political intervention into the present. With a deep commitment to defamiliarizing all we have come to take for granted, genealogy is a way to change the present through a turn to the past. Genealogy, after all, is *not* about the quest for origins but rather about the tracing of accidents, disparities, conflicts, and haphazard conditions, and this, Brown emphasizes, is how possibilities are pried open by genealogy: "If everything about us is the effect of historical accident rather than will or design, then we are paradoxically, both more severely historical and also more plastic that we might otherwise seem. We are more sedimented by history, but also more capable of intervening in our histories."[20] In short, genealogy "opens possibilities through which various futures might be pursued" and thereby crucially "*reduces the political need for progressive history as the only source of movement away from the present.*"[21] And this is one of the notable recurring themes of this book. What appears to make archives and archiving compelling to so many feminist activists who came of age after the crest of the second wave feminist movement is the fact that the archive, in a myriad of ways, opens up the possibility of being in time and in history differently.

That such a reorientation to history might be especially appealing to the displaced and disenchanted neoliberal subject is not surprising. Where history has been pushed into the past and the future supplanted by the sheer demands of the present, what could be more hopeful than the realization that time is not simply marching forward and that we might imagine a way outside our oppressive present *through* a radical repudiation of "progress"? This, I maintain, may also account for the archival turn in cultural theory, art, and activism since the early 1990s.

Despite their alleged purpose, archives are notoriously difficult, disorderly, impenetrable spaces, prone to produce multiple and conflicting narratives. "Gray, meticulous, and patiently documentary,"[22] the archive is where genealogy is arguably most visible and most frequently enacted. A turn toward the archive is not a turn toward the past but rather an essential way of understanding and imagining other ways to live in the present. In short, to the extent that archives render visible the "past of the present," they represent an integral step toward realizing a genealogical politics. As I emphasize throughout this book, this step may hold specific relevance for imagining a queer feminist politic at this particular political moment. As Elizabeth Freeman observes, women born during and after the rise of the second wave feminist movement came of age in the "afterlife of sixties" and are thereby "the successors to mass movements whose most radical elements were often tamed, crushed, or detoured into individualistic projects as they were disseminated through the mainstream media."[23] It follows that our "cultural debris" includes these "incomplete, partial or otherwise failed transformations of the social field."[24] Insofar as these failed transformations of the social field, however, can be reconfigured as spaces where political possibilities are made visible, even palpable, we affirm Brown's belief in the efficacy of a politics that turns to the past to unfix the terms of the present political situation. The archival turn under neoliberalism should not be primarily read as a desire to escape the present but rather as an attempt to regain agency in an era when the ability to collectively imagine and enact other ways of being in the world has become deeply eroded.

Feminist Cultural Production since 1990

As neoliberalism altered our relationship to time and history, the archive alternatively presented itself as a space of possibility—a way to think beyond the constraints of "progress" imposed by the neoliberal mindset. Indeed, although this study focuses primarily on feminist archives, archives have been taken up by a wide range of activist groups. Exemplary interventions range from the well-funded and high-profile ACT UP/NY Archives at the New York Public Library (and related ACT UP Oral History Project)[25] to far more DIY (do it yourself) initiatives, such as the Lower East Side Squatter and Homesteaders Archives that was started by a group of squatters and housing activists in a longstanding squat and with the support of a very modest grant of $1,845 from the Documentary Heritage Program.[26] As I maintain throughout this book, at least in the context of contemporary feminism, the relationship between neoliberalism and the archival turn may, however, also be accounted for on a more material level. Since the mid 1990s, the archive has presented itself not only as a conceptual space in which to rethink time, history, and progress against the grain of dominant ideologies but also as an apparatus through which to continue making and *legitimizing* forms of knowledge and cultural production that neoliberal restructuring otherwise renders untenable.

Above all, neoliberalism is committed to "liberating individual entrepreneurial freedoms" and upholding "the quality and integrity of money."[27] In a state where such objectives trump all other social and political goals, initiatives driven by anti-economic mandates (for example, collective projects privileging the production and dissemination of goods over profit-making) are naturally vulnerable. For this reason, it is by no means surprising that the rise of neoliberalism in the 1980s was accompanied by a sharp decline in feminist cultural production in the 1990s. As Barbara Godard observes, the explicitly anti-economic mandate of feminist cultural initiatives made such initiatives especially vulnerable to neoliberalism's strategy of "accumulation through dispossession."[28] Godard explains: "disavowal of profit also poses a potential for recuperation since, performed ever at a loss, women's altruistic labour is open to exploitation and further devaluation."[29] In other words, already committed to giving it away for free, the feminist culture sector was an easy target as the impact of neoliberal restructuring began to take its toll. Here, feminist publishing offers an especially illustrative example of neoliberalism's impact on both cultural and knowledge production. With neither overdetermining the impact of neoliberalism on the second wave feminist culture sector nor falsely implying that second wave feminist publishing necessarily disappeared in the early to mid 1990s, there is little doubt that from the late 1980s to mid 1990s, the feminist publishing industry,[30] which had been growing since the late 1960s, went through a sudden and sharp decline from which it has never recovered. Indeed, in 1989, Barbara Grier, in a letter announcing that there would be no Women in Print Conference that year, was still optimistic enough to send out a letter to her "Sister Publishers" predicting that "in five years we can probably plug the drain and make it financially, morally, spiritually, and logistically foolish beyond our comprehension for any woman writing in all our fields to go to other than a woman-owned publishing company or, at the very least, a small press rather than the trade press."[31] What Grier and her "sister publishers" could not have predicted in 1989 was that within five years most of the feminist publishers on the Women in Print mailing list would no longer exist, no longer exist as stand-alone publishers, or be struggling to survive in a radically transformed print economy. Despite the decline of the second wave feminist publishing industry in the 1990s, feminist cultural workers, scholars, and activists continued to publish, distribute, and legitimize their work throughout the decade and into the new millennium. The paradoxical "revival" of feminist publishing during its decline, I maintain, was at least partially carried out in and through the archive. To understand how the archive was used to revive feminist publishing in the 1990s, it is first necessary to consider the conditions underlying the second wave feminist publishing industry's decline in more detail.

In *Mixed Media: Feminist Presses and Publishing Politics*, Simone Murray presents feminist publishing as "the most consistently successful of women's interventions into media production since the 1960s."[32] Since 1990, however, most feminist publishing houses in North America and around the world have either collapsed or become imprints of larger, mainstream (that is, not "women owned") publishing houses.[33] It is ironic that the industry's initial grounds for expansion in the 1970s and 1980s also proved to be the primary reason for its rapid demise. The proliferation of feminist publishing houses during the early years of the women's liberation movement was largely driven by "a deeply ingrained suspicion of the multinational corporate publishing sector," which assumed that "women, carrying little policy-making weight in the managerial echelons of corporate publishing, risked having their writing co-opted and subsequently, dismissed as commercially passé as soon as the feminist 'trend' was deemed to have peaked."[34] To this end, "radical women's presses were characterized by non-hierarchical, collectivist structures, an emphasis on political engagement over profit generation, and a heightened self-consciousness of their position *vis-à-vis* the corporate mainstream."[35] The feminist publishing movement was not only committed to controlling who was involved in the production and distribution of texts; at least in the case of radical feminist publishing, there was a strong belief that cultural production must transform both the *process* and the *product*. As Trysh Travis's research on the "women in print" movement emphasizes, "The movement's largest goals were nothing short of revolutionary: it aimed to capture women's experiences and insights in durable—even beautiful—printed forms through a communications network free from patriarchal and capitalist control."[36] Describing second wave feminist printers and publishers as "book historians of the present," Travis further emphasizes the extent to which "women in print" activists took it upon themselves to analyze "late twentieth-century publishing institutions, the political economy that supported them, and the identitarian norms—in this case, norms of gender and sexuality—that inflected their workings."[37] The ability to understand the capitalist and patriarchal underpinnings of the book trade were integral to the feminist publishing industry's success in establishing, however briefly, an alternative print culture in the name of the women's movement. Such analysis, however, would ultimately prove inadequate in the face of neoliberal restructuring in the 1990s and beyond.

While at least some of the presses, publications, and distribution networks that were established in the 1970s to 1980s had understandably outgrown their mandates by the 1990s, many others were unable to survive the massive reorganization of the publishing industry and book trade that neoliberal restructuring put into motion. With specific reference to the United Kingdom, Murray observes, "throughout the 1980s and 1990s, British feminist publishers suffered under the economic rationalist cuts to public spending of the Thatcher, Major, and later, Blair, governments and were forced to seek alternative sources of funding in the wake of these governments' abolition or restructuring of grants-awarding bodies."[38] While public funding declined or entirely disappeared in most nations with extensive feminist publishing networks, including the UK, United States, Canada, and Australia, new obstacles also appeared in the book industry. Independent feminist bookstores—the primary distribution hub for feminist publishers—struggled to compete with the rise of "big box" book retailers, many with surprisingly large but not necessarily diverse Women's Studies, Queer Theory, and LGBT sections. At the same time, many small presses struggled to keep up with the demands these large retailers notoriously place on small presses to produce large print runs in order to fill orders for books that they often have little interest in either promoting or selling.[39] In this climate, the core mandates of feminist presses grew evermore out of touch with the reality of cultural production. Murray concludes that "the feminist priorities of political engagement, staff consciousness-raising, skills-sharing and the development of theoretical analysis pulled in the opposite direction from the quick decision-making, editorial individualism and financial opportunism that constitute prerequisites for survival in the competitive publishing realm."[40]

Surveying what remains of the feminist book industry today, there is little doubt that the industry was one of the many casualties of neoliberal restructuring. In short, as the space for imagining viable alternatives to profit-driven endeavors narrowed, cultural enterprises run on sweat equity and often at a deficit, such as feminist presses, became increasingly unimaginable. Yet, throughout the 1990s, as established venues to circulate feminist work were continuously slipping away, a new generation of feminist cultural workers and scholars *continued* to find ways to publish, disseminate, and even authorize their writing. The existence of feminist zine collections at Duke University's Sallie Bingham Center for Women's History and Culture and the Barnard College Library (two of the three archives and special collections featured in this book) reveal the scope and range of the feminist publishing movement that emerged as the second wave "women in print" movement went into decline. If publishing itself served as the central authorizing mechanism for second wave feminists, however, for a new generation of feminists, publishing, which would primarily take the form of "self-publishing," proved inadequate on its own. Thus, despite the fact that feminist zine producers, for example, shared much in common with their second wave counterparts[41]—most notably, an anti-economic mandate and commitment to revolutionizing cultural production at the level of process and product—their writing initially eluded recognition both outside and inside the feminist movement.[42] What is now apparent is that neither the decline of the small press and the broader feminist culture sector in the early 1990s nor the initial lack of recognition from their feminist elders prevented these women from finding ways to legitimize their voices and gain symbolic currency. In fact, in the long run, their strategy may prove even more enduring than their feminist foremothers' deployment of print-based economies.

If feminist zines and other self-published and self-produced forms of feminist cultural production from the 1990s have not only survived but also gained legitimacy as works of literature, art, and knowledge, it is to the extent that these works, produced outside the framework of an established culture industry, rapidly migrated to archives and special collections. The inception of Riot Grrrl is most often dated to 1990. By the late 1990s, Sarah Dyer was in negotiations with archivists at Duke University about the possibility of donating thousands of zines, many directly linked to the Riot Grrrl movement, to the Sallie Bingham Center for Women's History and Culture, a center housed in their rare book and manuscript library. Dyer's subsequent donation in 2000 represented only the first of many donations to Duke University. As this book explores, however, in the early years of the new millennium, major collections of feminist documents and self-published materials were established at university libraries across North America.

Although professional archivists understandably worry about the increasingly hazy distinction between the terms "collection," "library," and "archive,"[43] to label a personal collection an "archive" and, more significantly, to place a personal collection in an established archive remains a powerful authorizing act and *not* because either act is necessarily committed to preservation. When Foucault refers to the archive in *The Order of Things*, it is first and foremost as a "system" invested with the power to "establish statements as events ... and things."[44] For Foucault, the archive is an authorizing apparatus—a structure that determines which statements can and do *act* in and upon the world. As emphasized throughout this book, precisely the recognition of the archive as discursive structure has driven the archival turn in contemporary feminist activism, scholarship, and cultural production. For a generation or two of women born during and following the rise of the second wave feminist movement, inaugurating private and semipublic collections as archives and donating them to established public and university archives and special collections is central to how they legitimize their voices in the public sphere. In this sense, archives serve the same function served by a previous generation's alternative print economy. The archive, in this respect, arguably strengthens contemporary feminism not only as a space of possibility to the extent that it is a scene for the realization of a genealogical politics but also, more practically, as a necessary and effective authorizing apparatus in an economy that is hostile to the production and circulation of works produced quite literally at the cost of profit.

Archival Order, Dirty Methods

As emphasized above, the archival turn in contemporary feminism is neither simply part of a larger turn to the archive in cultural theorizing and art nor simply the result of a longing for the past. Thus, understanding the archival turn in contemporary feminism demands an analysis that is as attentive to history as it is to the present economic and political terrain. As a result, this book is informed by empirical research (both archival and ethnographic) and by theoretical interrogations of these research traditions. Before further elaborating on my research methodology, however, it is important to at least briefly consider how my relationship to the communities and materials at the center of this book also shaped its development.

The Archival Turn in Feminism did not begin as the result of a research decision but rather as the result of an accident. Because I have been at least peripherally linked to the communities at the center of this book and, more important, because somewhere along the line I chose to collect the debris of these communities, I was eventually forced to do something with the ephemera accumulating around me. The ephemera in question, which included Riot Grrrl zines and LPs, lesbian feminist porn magazines, radical feminist books and newspapers, and a nearly complete print run of the *Lesbian Ladder* (items variously acquired through my research, as "donations" from older colleagues, or through successful bids on eBay), had become a burden. Too copious to move from place to place but too valuable to toss away, I turned to the archive for a practical solution. When I began to look for an appropriate institutional home for my personal collection I discovered that my desire to collect the material traces of my own generation of feminists alongside an earlier generation's ephemeral legacies, as well as my desire to resituate my personal archive in an institutional context, was by no means unique. In essence, this book began with a desire to off-load the history accumulating around me (or at least to off-load its material traces), but, in my bid to do away with history, I found myself reoriented to the past.

What I have produced here, of course, is not a history. If it is anything that resembles history, then at best it is what Brown describes as "dirty history"—a history that will never be at home among "histories of reason, meaning, or higher purposes" but only among "histories of varied and protean orders of subjection."[45] In short, this book's only stake in history is in exposing how it is made and to what ends. For all these reasons, my approach is anything but orthodox. Although this book is primarily comprised of three "case studies" on archives, my work in these archives was approached not as a historian but, more precisely, as an ethnographer and cultural theorist with an interest in the production, circulation, and use of texts as well as the production and writing of histories. Like my history, then, my methodology is also a bit "dirty" or perhaps simply queer. As Judith Halberstam observes, this is by no means unique in the realm of queer methodology. Queer researchers, after all, have a tendency to display "a certain disloyalty to conventional disciplinary methods."[46] Whether dirty or queer, "methodological disloyalty" *is* an apt way to summarize my approach here. Among other methods, this book is informed by participant observations carried out in archives and special collections where I was simultaneously engaged in archival research. This book is also informed by interviews with some of the archivists, librarians, researchers, and donors I met or discovered as a result of my archival research. Finally, and more important, this book is informed by overlapping and interdisciplinary approaches to the study of history that take as their starting points a deep skepticism about history's claim to truth and transcendence. Yet, however impure or dirty my methods may be here, this book does build on at least two established research traditions. *The Archival Turn in Feminism* extends a tradition of feminist book and publishing history research, most often associated with the groundbreaking work of Janice Radway in the early 1980s, which brings ethnographic approaches to bear on the study of texts and textual communities.[47] At the same time, this study is part of a more recent and growing tendency among historians, sociologists, and cultural studies scholars to bring ethnographic methods to bear on the study of archives to "denaturalize the presumptive boundaries of official archive space."[48]

If I am guilty of deploying dirty or queer methods in the creation of this book, however, then I am equally guilty of approaching the subject of archives and special collections as a cultural theorist. As my archivist and librarian colleagues are quick to point out, under the archival turn, the concept of the archive has all but lost its specificity. Like many cultural theorists interested in archives, I admit that I am partially responsible for the archive's semantic drift. Throughout the past decade, I have published articles and presented papers that apply the term archive to collections as varied as recipe boxes and databases. As someone who is also frequently called upon to review articles on the subject of archives, I have assessed articles that apply the concept of the archive to even more varied subjects—the most absurd of which was recycled laundromat water. As John Ridener rightly observes, for archivists, "A mixed response to postmodern criticism is logical since much of postmodernism's viability as an overarching philosophy is debatable."[49] Although my own approach to the subject of archives is deeply informed by cultural theory, it is also deeply informed by my dialogues and collaborations with feminist archivists and special collections librarians, many of whom feature in this book. On this account, *The Archival Turn in Feminism* departs from many other books on the archive originating in Cultural Studies and its related fields. In *An Archive of Feelings*, for example, Cvetkovich uses the term "archive" in reference to community-based collections, such as the Lesbian Herstory Archives, but primarily uses the term more loosely in reference to an entire spectrum of broadly conceived collections, including those found in films (for example, Cheryl Dunye's film *The Watermelon Woman*) and even describes her own book as one structured as "an archive."[50] In *In A Queer Time & Place*, Halberstam calls on queer activists and scholars to reimagine the archive as a sort of "floating signifier" and in the process casts the archive's net wide enough to include just about any form of accumulation. At the same time, Halberstam maintains that the archive must exceed its current definition as a repository of documents and be understood as "a theory of cultural relevance, a construction of collective memory, and a complex record."[51] In Diana Taylor's *The Archive and the Repertoire*, the archive is recast as something that is by no means more enduring or permanent than the repertoire of lived experience and thereby as something no longer bound by its status as a repository of concrete materials. On many levels, my own theorizing on archives is informed by and supports the approach exemplified by Cvetkovich, Halberstam, Taylor, and other cultural theorists who have taken up the archive as a subject of inquiry over the past decade. Indeed, to the extent that queer and feminist archives have by necessity so often developed outside or on the edges of established archival spaces, including those associated with the state and the university, and frequently developed in response to emotional rather than strictly intellectual needs,[52] to limit my discussion of archives to those that meet the strictest archival standards would be to foreclose the possibility of fully investigating how feminist archives have taken shape. That said, I maintain that, if cultural theorists wish to investigate the archive, it is by no means fruitful to simply ignore professional definitions and standards concerning the archive.

Thus, while my approach is by no means entirely uncontaminated by cultural theory's "loose" nomenclature, which has at times implied that the archive refers simply to "traces of the past collected either intentionally or haphazardly as 'evidence,'"[53] I have attempted to use the terms "archive" and "special collection" as faithfully as possible. My audience, after all, includes cultural theorists, specifically those working in and across the fields of Cultural Studies, Literary Studies, Book and Publishing History, and Gender and Sexuality Studies, as well as professional archivists and librarians. Therefore, while I do not pretend to offer practical advice to those charged with the extraordinary challenge of collecting and preserving documents in established archives and special collections, I am committed to offering insights that may be at least relevant to these frontline workers in their attempt to think through the broader political and cultural implications of their day-to-day labor. Although scholars frequently depict libraries, special collections, and archives as arbitrary and aleatory spaces where materials simply surface, such dismissive assumptions erase the complex work of professional librarians and archivists. Indeed, as Freedman argues, materials don't "simply 'surface'—it's not random or chaotic—librarians and archivists work really hard to help that stuff get out there," and this is precisely where activism enters their profession. As such, it is also my hope that this book might prompt my own colleagues, who are invariably reliant on the work of professional archivists and librarians but more often than not know little about the intellectual and practical challenges they face on the job, to also take more seriously the theoretical insights of information professionals.

The Archival Turn in Feminism is comprised of five chapters. Chapter 1, "The 'Scrap Heap' Reconsidered: Selected Archives of Feminist Archiving," builds on the discussion advanced in this introduction, which understands the archival turn as a realization of genealogical politics. In addition to offering a partial history of feminist archiving (a history that begins during the decline of first wave feminist activism), this chapter examines how a younger generation's apparent nostalgia for the ideologies, practices, and cultural artifacts of a previous generation's "women's liberation" movement has structured the development of many contemporary collections of feminist texts, artifacts, and papers. Following Elizabeth Freeman, however, I do not necessarily posit this turn back to 1970s feminism as "pure nostalgia for another revolutionary moment" but rather as an attempt to mine "the present for signs of undetonated energy from past revolutions."[54] Thus, in sharp contrast to many feminist commentaries, such as Susan Faludi's theory of "feminism's ritual matricide," which reinforces the perception that contemporary feminism is irreparably marked by intergenerational conflict, I maintain that what continues to make feminism relevant to women born during and after the rise of the second wave feminist movement is precisely their preoccupation with an earlier generation's histories of struggles—a dynamic that is most visibly being enacted in and through the archive.

The following three chapters each take the form of a "case study" of a specific archive or special collection. Each case study is concerned with the various ways in which the development of these archives and special collections opens up the possibility to tell different types of stories about feminism's recent history while simultaneously rendering visible previously obscured narratives about feminism. Building on the analysis advanced in the introductory chapters, chapter 2, "Archival Regeneration," examines how the zine collections at Duke University's Sallie Bingham Center for Women's History and Culture provide a context in which to explore the continuities—in content, design, and form—between second wave feminist and Riot Grrrl and third wave feminist publications. Drawing on interviews with Collections Development Librarian Kelly Wooten and donors, most notably Sarah Dyer (who donated the first and largest of the zine collections housed at Duke University), this chapter pays specific attention to how archival collections, which create intentional and sometimes unintentional proximities between the cultural and intellectual products of different generations, open up opportunities to reimagine the possibilities of feminist storytelling. Following Clare Hemmings's call for feminists to learn how to "tell stories differently" in order to avoid repeating false claims to truth about feminism and some of the political pitfalls that have hampered Western feminism over the past four decades, chapter 2 explores the role of archives and archiving in this urgent work.

Remaining focused on the relationship between archives, archiving, and storytelling, chapter 3, "Redefining a Movement," examines the more recent development of the Riot Grrrl Collection at NYU's Fales Library and Special Collections. Based on interviews with the collection's senior archivist, Lisa Darms, and several donors, including Kathleen Hanna and Johanna Fateman, this chapter examines how the archivization of Riot Grrrl materials holds the potential to rewrite the history of Riot Grrrl. Specifically, chapter 3 advances two connected arguments about contemporary feminism and archives. First, this chapter examines how—two decades after Riot Grrrl's development—the women most synonymous with Riot Grrrl are using the archive to resituate the movement as one more deeply aligned with second wave feminist theory, continental philosophy, and avant-garde literary and art traditions than youth subcultures. Second, with specific reference to Pierre Bourdieu's theorizing on the field of cultural production and to feminist critiques of his theorizing, this chapter further examines the archive's role in "position-takings." Chapter 3 specifically explores how the Riot Grrrl Collection demonstrates the archive's potential to be deployed as an apparatus through which one might retroactively *take a position* in the field of cultural production that was hitherto denied.

In chapter 4's final case study, "Radical Catalogers and Accidental Archivists," I turn my attention to the Barnard Zine Library and to the activist librarianship of the collection's founder, Jenna Freedman. Although Freedman is engaged in the development of a special collection and parallel archival collection, it is notable that her primary site of activism is not the collection itself but rather the library catalog where she creates points of access for the subjects and perspectives found in the zines at the center of her collection. With reference to the history of radical librarianship, collecting, and cataloging by which Freedman is deeply influenced, chapter 4 demonstrates how contemporary activist librarians, through their tactical interventions at the level of the library catalog, are altering the visibility of otherwise marginal knowers and knowledges. None of the collections featured in this book has an explicit mandate to collect born-digital materials or to digitize printed materials. In fact, all of the archives and special collections featured in the following chapters have, at different points, adopted mandates to focus on the collection and preservation of material documents and artifacts rather than born-digital materials and further concluded that digitization is not an immediate priority. In this third case study, I further argue that this may reflect a recognition that item-level cataloging of marginal materials holds more potential for subversion than simply digitizing the same materials.

Throughout *The Archival Turn in Feminism*, I examine how the structure and mandate of the collections in question are effectively resituating contemporary feminist cultural production and knowledge. I also explore the specific political, cultural, and intellectual mandates of the archivists and librarians responsible for the collections. In the concluding chapter 5, I further grapple with the seemingly contradictory movement of activist collections to archives and libraries at private universities. I consider specifically whether this movement simply reflects a cooptation of radical histories, or rather is consistent with the contradictions that have always structured the development of feminist activist collections.

Above all else, *The Archival Turn in Feminism* seeks to locate archiving and librarianship as forms of applied theorizing with far-reaching implications for activism and scholarship in the twenty-first century and to take seriously the possibility of the archive and special collection as central rather than peripheral sites of resistance.

1 / The "Scrap Heap" Reconsidered: Selected Archives of Feminist Archiving

Feminism's heritage is repeatedly hurled onto the scrap heap.
—SUSAN FALUDI, "American Electra:
Feminism's Ritual Matricide"

*Now I think the point may be to trail behind actually exist-
ing social possibilities: to be interested in the tail end of things,
willing to be bathed in the fading light of whatever has been
declared useless.*
—ELIZABETH FREEMAN, *Time Binds:
Queer Temporalities, Queer Histories*

In October 2010, Susan Faludi published an article in *Harper's Magazine* on the subject of "feminism's ritual matricide." In summary, Faludi argues that American feminism has always been and remains structured by a matricidal impulse. Feminism's self-inflicted death drive not only derives a long history but also, according to Faludi, permeates nearly all aspects of feminist practice and theory. In keeping with her previous polemics on feminism, she targets "academic" feminism and what she more specifically and variously describes as "poststructuralist" or "postmodern" feminism as the primary culprits. In the following passage, her argument is laid bare for *Harper's* readers:

> [The] academic motherlode is in danger of being decommissioned by the increasing disconnect between practical, political feminism and academic feminist theory, and by the rise of a poststructuralist philosophy in gender studies that prefers the deconstructing of female experience to the linkages and legacies of women's history and regards generational dynamics, and even the categories of "woman"

and "man," as artifices to perform and discard. These two legacies—the continued matricide and the shape-shifting contamination of commercialism and commercially infused relativism in feminist activism and scholarship—have created a generational donnybrook where the transmission of power repeatedly fails and feminism's heritage is repeatedly hurled onto the scrap heap. What gets passed on is the predisposition to dispossess, a legacy of no legacy.[1]

In just a few sentences, Faludi expresses a set of assumptions about contemporary feminism that this book directly calls into question. She claims that the so-called "academic motherlode" (women's studies or gender studies) is at risk owing to the "increasing disconnect between practical, political feminism and academic feminist theory"; she thereby implies that the threat to feminist scholarship is internal conflict rather than external factors, including the far-reaching effects of neoliberal restructuring on the feminist culture sector and more general impact on higher education. She further assumes that somewhere in a mythical feminist past, praxis, politics, and theory *were* connected or at least more so than they are in the present. Finally, and most significantly, Faludi assumes that feminism's heritage has been "repeatedly hurled onto the scrap heap." Our legacy, she concludes, is one marked by a complete rejection of our history.

By the time Faludi's *Harper's* article was forwarded to me by a colleague, I had already encountered her latest theory on the state of contemporary feminism. Faludi had tested the argument at a 2010 conference hosted by the Gender Studies Program at The New School.[2] Listening to Faludi's talk, I was struck by its incompatibility with my own experience of and research on contemporary feminism. While Faludi, a self-appointed spokeswoman for the feminist movement since the early 1990s, may be unable to imagine women of different generations knowing each other outside the lens of mother-daughter relationships—with all the psychic and social baggage traditional family relationships entail—as a queer woman, my intergenerational relationships with women have never been confined to such familial roles. The older women in my life, both queer and straight, have been just as likely to assume the roles of terrifying mentor, embarrassing crush, or quirky friend as they have been to stand in as mothers, and none of these relationships has been first and foremost defined by conflict, let alone incited thoughts of "ritual matricide." Even when I have resented the advice or rejected the politics of my "elders," I have remained fiercely protective of what they represent and grateful for everything they have made possible in my personal and professional life. For this reason, I have taken great interest, even pleasure, in combing their "scrap heap," which has variously served as my research material, my entertainment, and sometimes my template for imagining other ways of being in the world.

For many years, I worried that my fondness for earlier eras of feminist and especially queer feminist activism, writing, and cultural production was not only theoretically and politically problematic but also my own dirty little secret. At some point early in the new millennium, however, I found myself increasingly accompanied in my pining for an era of ideas and politics I am too young to have experienced firsthand. What began as off-the-record exchanges with other women born since the late 1960s about our secret stashes of radical feminist literature and women's lib music soon escalated into public art exhibits and academic panels dedicated to exploring an earlier era of feminism from the perspective of *not* being there. And as explored throughout this book, this historical turn would eventually result in the establishment of several major feminist collections that seek to preserve my own generation's activism and cultural production but in ways that persistently seek to align this work with legacies of feminist activism and cultural production while simultaneously placing these legacies in a new light. In *Time Binds: Queer Temporalities, Queer Histories*, a book-length study exploring the work of a generation of queer feminist artists born since the mid 1960s, Elizabeth Freeman describes this phenomenon as a form of "temporal drag." Associating temporal drag with "retrogression, delay, and the pull of the past on the present,"[3] she offers the concept as a way of "connecting queer performativity to disavowed political histories," especially the disavowed history of lesbian feminism. Central to Freeman's discussion of temporal drag is a rethinking of generational dynamics outside the framework of the family: "The concept of generations linked by political work or even mass entertainment also acknowledges the ability of various technologies and culture industries to produce shared subjectivities that go beyond the family."[4] Throughout her study, Freeman provides examples of contemporary feminist artists engaging directly with the ideas and iconography of their radical foremothers, but, as she observes, in the work of these artists "the 1970s emerge as the scene of mass socialist, feminist, and gay-liberationists projects retrospectively loved or hated but also used as placeholders for thinking beyond the status quo of the 1990s and early years of the twenty-first century."[5] In other words, for these artists, the past is something neither to reject nor to accept without question, since they are ultimately engaged in "mining the present for signs of undetonated energy from past revolutions."[6]

The gap between Faludi, with her sweeping generalizations about the "scrap heap" onto which feminist histories are repeatedly hurled, and Freeman, with her open admission that the "point may be to trail behind actually existing social possibilities: to be interested in the tail end of things, willing to be bathed in the fading light of whatever has been declared useless,"[7] is a gap not easily bridged. But Faludi and Freeman also live in different worlds and perhaps, more precisely, different times, and these differences are by no means inconsequential. Faludi's inability to recognize that contemporary feminism may be structured by a longing, even nostalgia, for previous eras of feminism rather than by a radical repudiation of feminist histories, as she suggests, is by no means unrelated to her understanding of time and history as concepts necessarily structured along the lines of the traditional heterosexual family with its inherent temporal linearity and Electra-inspired dramas. Similarly, Freeman's ability to recognize that something radically different was underway in the 1990s, even as popular accounts of feminism were actively promoting a narrative of generational divide, is by no means unrelated to her understanding of time and history as concepts that can be unbound from traditional notions of the family and history's assumed teleological tendencies. Important in the context of this discussion is that assumptions about time and history deeply shape one's perception of the feminist "scrap heap." As Freeman observes, for most of the artists featured in her study, whose childhoods unfolded at the height of the second wave feminist movement, the 1970s "glimmer forth as an embarrassment," "something that remains to be rethought."[8] In other words, what is cast away is not simply rejected. The scrap heap, then, is not a site of refuse/refusal but a complex site where the past accumulates in the present as a resource to be embraced and rejected, mined and recycled, discarded and redeployed. As such, feminism's scrap heap is both a site of abjection—that which must be expelled but that which we cannot live without—and simultaneously a playground, a refuge, a scene of innovation, humor, hope, and longing. In every respect, feminism's scrap heap is integral rather than superfluous, vital rather than stagnant.

I raise Freeman's study here because in many respects the subjects of her study (feminist and queer visual artists born during and since the 1960s) share much in common with the subjects of my own study (mostly queer, feminist archivists, librarians and DIY collectors born since the 1960s). To be clear, this is *not* to imply that the collections and collectors at the center of this book are necessarily queer. The collections under consideration here are first and foremost defined by their feminist rather than queer content. Yet, if I may, however cautiously, unmoor "queer" from its status as a sexual identity and practice and think about it more along the lines of Judith Halberstam who posits queer as something that ultimately refers to "non-normative logics and organizations of community, sexual identity, embodiment, and activity in space and time," there *is* something very queer about the orientation of these collections. Where their queerness resides, however, has much less to do with representation and more to do with the tacit but by no means insignificant relationship to time and history that these collections express and enact. What makes these collections queer is a relationship to time and history that recognizes the utter contingency, even fragility, of eras, epochs, and events and further recognizes how uncannily present the present may be in the past. What makes these collections queer, then, is that they recognize not only the possibility but also the necessity of what Carolyn Dinshaw describes as "making relations with the past."[9] The queerness of these collections, therefore, resides in their remarkable ability to be in time differently—to recognize the past as a way to reinvigorate a beleaguered present and to recognize the future as always already implicated by the pull of the past. In this respect, the queerness of these collections both reflects the queerness of the collections at the center of Ann Cvetkovich's study, *An Archive of Feelings*, which posits queer archives as archives of "emotion and trauma" and exceeds the bounds of Cvetkovich's definition.[10] If the queer archives discussed by Cvetkovich as well as other theorists of queer time and history, such as Halberstam, have tended to be primarily characterized as idiosyncratic, the queerness of the collections in this study is defined along somewhat different grounds.[11] Here, queer appears as a concept that is *neither* necessarily resistant to order *nor* necessarily incompatible with established institutions but rather as a concept that is simply resistant to existing orders and entrenched institutional ways of operating.

I want to avoid, however, implying that the collections under consideration in this book are necessarily unique in the history of feminist archives and collections. Although what might be properly described as "women's archives" or "women's collections" have long been governed by the teleological assumptions upon which most archival collections are structured, there is nothing necessarily teleological about the development of explicitly feminist archives and special collections. Indeed, these "scrap heaps" of documents and artifacts suggest an orientation to "queer time" long before such a concept came into circulation. I make this claim on at least two bases. Feminist archives and special collections initially developed during a period of seemingly irreparable decline rather than political progress for feminists. In this sense, feminist archives and special collections have always already been rooted in the assumption that political progress, no matter how entrenched, is ultimately a chimera. Equally important is the recognition that many of these collections—at least those with a focus on feminist politics rather than simply female subjects—have long been as concerned with the promotion and development of feminist culture in the present as they have been with the preservation of past achievements. In short, feminist archives and special collections—even those connected to established institutions—have, since their earliest incarnation, exhibited a strong tendency to exceed preservationist objectives, thereby challenging expectations and understandings of the archive broadly defined.

In this chapter, I consider some conditions under which feminist archives have developed. Rather than provide a history of feminist archives, however, my objective is to place the archival turn in contemporary feminism in a historical context and to seriously consider how understandings of queer time and history might enable to us to better understand this turn. In this chapter, I ask what might be gained from considering the place of archives and archiving in contemporary feminist activism and knowledge production. I specifically maintain that drawing our attention to the archival turn in contemporary feminism is one way to move beyond the generational debates that have stifled feminist activism and scholarship since the 1990s—one way to counter the narrative that Faludi and other critics continue to promote about contemporary feminism and its discontents. Indeed, building on my discussion of "genealogical politics" laid out in the Introduction, I propose that examining the archival turn in contemporary feminism is one way to take seriously the politically efficacy of failed social transformations and abandoned revolutions.

The Archives of Feminist Archiving

As already emphasized, my intent is not to identify when and where feminist archives began. To do so, I would need to account for the DIY collectors who were accumulating traces of their activism in the late nineteenth and early twentieth centuries but not necessarily in the context of institutional collections (for example, university archives). I would also need to account for an entire range of "archival genres,"[12] such as scrapbooks, which offer glimpses into how women were collecting and documenting their involvement in public life prior to the establishment of feminist collections. Rather than attempt to provide a comprehensive history of feminist archiving, I turn my attention to two early efforts to collect and preserve traces of the feminist movement, paying specific attention to the continuities between these early collections and the collections at the center of this study.

The development of women's collections and more specifically, feminist collections is not, as one might expect, a product of first wave feminism in the early twentieth century but the more notable product of its subsequent decline. In the introduction to *Women's Collections: Libraries, Archives and Consciousness*, Suzanne Hildenbrand observes, "Paradoxically, many major women's collections of today can trace their origins to periods of low interest in feminism."[13] Hildenbrand further observes that "the 1930s and 1940s saw a remarkable trend towards the establishment of women's collections, as veterans of the feminist campaigns of the early twentieth century anxiously sought institutional homes for their private papers, and other materials they had collected, in a world suddenly disinterested in, or hostile to, the cause to which they had devoted their lives."[14] Most notable of these developments were two projects initiated in 1935: the World Center for Women's Archives (WCWA) in New York and the International Archives for the Women's Movement (IAV) in Amsterdam. Like the story of the feminist movement, however, neither archive's development was simply marked by progress. To illustrate, I first consider the story of the WCWA.

The WCWA was launched in 1935 by Rosika Schwimmer, a Hungarian-born but stateless feminist activist. In a 1935 letter Schwimmer announced the idea for the archive: "Women's international efforts and achievements for equal social, political and economic rights in the course of the last century were at their peak during the first years which followed the World War," but "retrogression set in when, as the aftermath of war, many nations became victims of dictatorships and when the economic crisis spread over the world."[15] She was well aware of the impact of her era's political and economic crisis on not only women's progress but also on the visibility of early feminist activism, which was increasingly being placed under erasure in the historical record. Indeed, she appeared acutely aware of the extent to which archiving past feminist accomplishments was integral to achieving contemporary political goals: "It is at this period of retrogression in women's rights and pacifist activities that it becomes of utmost importance to assemble the facts of women's struggle and achievements during the last century at least, so the at historians of the future will find it possible to establish the truth about today."[16] Schwimmer realized early on, however, that her goal of establishing what she originally conceived of as an archive of feminist pacifist activism was not a goal she could achieve alone, and she persuaded historian Mary Beard of the need to establish the archive.

With Beard on board, the idea for the archive expanded in scope from feminist pacifist activism to feminist activism in general, while still upholding Schwimmer's central political mandate. It is significant that the idea for the archive was never simply rooted in a desire to preserve past accomplishments but instead was bound up in an urgent need to create an archive that might also serve as a catalyst for feminist activism in the present: "Seminars, teaching, public lectures, sharing of research on women, and the task of linking scholarship and activism were to be features of the archives."[17] In reality, by the time the organization was established, the idea that the WCWA would also house a school (a concept that anticipated the establishment of the first Women's Studies program by more than three decades) appears to have been sidelined. Nevertheless, the vision expressed in the founding committee's initial letter to donors, signed by members Mary Beard, Dr. Kathryn McHale, Mary Jobson, Lena Madesin Phillips, and Geline MacDonald Bow, carried forward the spirit of an archive with a broad mandate to support feminist activism in the present and to educate future generations of women and men:

> Believing that Mme. Schwimmer's proposal for a Women's Archives Center . . . has a value not only for historians who will help mold opinion in the future about the woman of today but a value also for the present generation of young men and women, we the undersigned have undertaken to set the ball rolling for sponsors of this project. . . . But we want more than shelves filled with records. It is our idea to make this Center a vital educational plant in which the culture represented by the archives will receive the attention at present given in "seats of higher learning" to the culture of men alone. By this agency we hope to provide an *equal education* which is sadly lacking now.[18]

From 1935 to 1939, the WCWA continued to gather support and expand its reach, both through the endorsement of high-profile sponsors, from Eleanor Roosevelt to Georgia O'Keeffe, and by forging connections with established libraries, universities, and other women's and girls organizations.[19] In a 1939 pamphlet entitled "Brief Report of World Center for Women's Archives," the WCWA outlined the "Need for a Women's Archive":

> In the beginning the mere idea was all that could be advanced. The idea was so new as to be revolutionary to the thought of women and men. The public at large did not realize the extent to which history had eliminated the story of women. Existing institutions, even women's colleges,

tended to specialize in men's materials. They had very little source material of any kind because women themselves
were inclined to destroy their own documents while carefully preserving the letters or other materials of their father
and brothers. And women who had been active in public
affairs of all kinds were inclined to destroy their records,
believing them of no account to others or because of mod-
esty. . . . Many women expressed a doubt that women's
materials could be found in private hands. In short, American women four years ago did not seem to be history-
minded with respect to their own sex. They were inclined
to ignore or belittle their women's heritage and to forget
that the keepers of records are guardians of civilization and
culture for generations to come.[20]

Continuing under the subheading, "Change In Thought
Effected," the same pamphlet reflected upon the WCWA's progress since 1935:

Now, within four years, a fundamental change in thought
has been effected. And through the leadership of World
Center for Women's Archives a triple entente has been
developing. Its components are: 1) source materials providing a wider and deeper knowledge of women; 2) a keener
understanding of the educational problem on college campuses; and 3) positive efforts on the part of broadcasting
systems to enlighten the audiences of the air about wom-
en's participation in the making of history, civilization, and
culture.[21]

Although the WCWA was a print-based collection, it was
deeply in tune with the emerging media technologies of the
era. In fact, Mary Beard and several other women directly connected to the WCWA played a major role in the production
of the groundbreaking 1939 NBC radio series, "Women in the
Making of America."[22] The organization's interest in emerging forms of broadcasting reveals that they were aware of the

fact that their efforts needed to do much more than preserve women's past accomplishments in existing formats. In short, they recognized that however essential an archive may be, they needed to be just as deeply engaged in promoting the status of women in the present. Creating radio programs about the history of women was one effort among many to establish an archive that was as contemporaneous as it was oriented to the past. Such efforts also supported the organization's ambition to "dramatize the center" through high-profile activities.

The WCWA, however, was not merely the impetus of a group of first wave feminists in the United States who had grown worried about their own legacies. An immigrant herself, Schwimmer had connections to feminist activists in Europe and subsequently was aware that the archive could also operate as a powerful instrument of state control. By the mid 1930s, archival technologies, broadly defined, were being used to identify and separate the population across Europe. In 1936, Josef Franz Knöpfler, the director of the Bavarian archival administration, emphasized the importance of "the mobilization of documents, which indicate the origin and development of race and people" and concluded that "there is no racial politics without archives, without archivists."[23] The archives would not only play an essential role in the identification and eventual segregation and detainment of the Jewish population but consequently determine who had the right to access public archives and keep private ones. By 1938, members of the Jewish community were prohibited from using German archives.[24] As the Jewish community fled or were forced to move to smaller living quarters, many archives and libraries were abandoned. By the end of the war, nearly all private Jewish archives and libraries had been pillaged and destroyed or sacrificed by their owners. As Peter Fritzsche observes, in Nazi Germany "the possession of the archive itself became the arbiter of historical existence."[25]

The WCWA emerged not simply as a liberatory project spearheaded by American feminists to secure their own legacies of activism, then, but as a necessary and urgent response to the archive's deployment as an instrument of genocide. In their initial 1935 letter announcing the archive's development, the committee's founding members observe: "Hitler is now shouting in the world that equality is no basis for the State. In this Center we may demonstrate that equality is a firm foundation for the state."[26] Although their initiative would not succeed in this respect, evidence shows that it did shelter at least some documentation that would have otherwise been abandoned or destroyed. In the 1939 pamphlet, the organization acknowledges that in addition to the donations of women in the United States, "Women of Europe are also responding to an appeal to send their documents for safe keeping before they are destroyed."[27]

It is important to emphasize, however, that in Europe another feminist archival project was also well under way. Like the WCWA, the International Archives for the Women's Movement (IAV) was initially propelled by the passion of a single activist—in this case, Rosa Manus.[28] The parallels between Schwimmer and Manus are worth noting. Manus, one of three founders of the archive, was also a Jewish woman who had been actively involved in both feminist and peace activism in the early part of the twentieth century. Moreover, her decision to establish the archive in the mid 1930s reflected a realization that the history of feminist activism was already being placed under erasure.[29] But in Manus's case, the decision was also personal. In 1929, Aletta Jacobs, the first female doctor in the Netherlands, passed away and left her papers to Manus. In the process, Jacobs unintentionally planted the seed for the establishment of a feminist archive in the Netherlands.[30] The archive would not take shape, however, until Manus met Willemijn Posthumus-van der Goot, a Dutch economist with a personal connection to two other archival projects (the Netherlands Economic History Archive and International Institute of Social History (IISH), both founded by her husband). Following a consultation by Posthumus with the founders of the IISH, Manus, Posthumus, and Johanna W. A. Naber (a founding member of the International Women's

Suffrage Alliance) founded the IAV in December 1935—the same year the WCWA was established in the United States.[31]

In many respects, the IAV and WCWA led parallel lives on opposite sides of the Atlantic in the mid to late 1930s. At the IAV's official opening in 1936, Posthumus emphasized the archive's role as both a repository of documents and a producer of new scholarly publications that would contribute to a "better understanding of the women's movement."[32] In addition to its desire to be engaged in both the collection and production of feminist documents, the IAV, like the WCWA, was also international in scope. Shortly after its founding, it established an international advisory board to help ensure this mandate. In a 1937 memorandum, the IAV articulated the global and ambitious scope of their project:

> The I.A.V. which is *the first and only institution* of its kind in the world, has a very high conception of its task of *international coordination,* the more so as they are convinced that a better and *centralized* organisation of the Women's Movement throughout the world is not only of scientific importance but is also apt greatly to strengthen international friendship and thereby add to the maintenance of peaceful relations.[33]

By 1940, the IAV had acquired the papers of a number of Dutch women's organizations and well-known feminist activists, approximately 4500 books and brochures, including valuable first editions of works by notable feminist writers, such as Mary Wollstonecraft, and a unique collection of 150 contemporary feminist journals from at least twenty countries.[34]

The parallels between the IAV and WCWA were not restricted to the founding members' common backgrounds nor to the work carried out by the two archives in the mid to late 1930s. Both archives also came to an abrupt halt in late 1939 to early 1940. The first blow surprisingly befell the US-based WCWA. In fact, only a few months after the publication of the 1939 pamphlet in which they celebrated the archive's role in safekeeping the papers of Jewish women in Europe, Inez Haynes Irwin, writing on behalf of the archive, announced the WCWA's collapse due to the outbreak of the war. As the final correspondence related to the archive makes clear, resources to support a project of this nature simply could no longer be secured: "Although it has been hard sledding, we have managed to get along until the present violent world situation manifested itself. Now it is almost impossible to raise money for anything outside the charities connected with the War and the evacuations."[35] Despite conceding that the archive would never be established as envisioned by Schwimmer and the other original members, Irwin expressed optimism that the archive would eventually be realized in some form at some time:

> We can not believe that a project of such magnitude and importance as the preservation of women's archives will die. We believe that running underground during these years of our concentration on the sinister events in the upper world, ultimately the idea will burst forth here, there, everywhere. When the quiet days of peace and reconstruction come, we are sure there will be many such organizations we have worked so hard to form and perhaps ultimately the big central one that was our dream.[36]

The "big central one" that the members of the WCWA dreamt of establishing would never be realized, but the materials collected in their initial effort would play a significant role in promoting the establishment of women's collections and feminist collections at several colleges. Following the organization's collapse, most of the materials fell into the hands of Mary Beard. While some materials were returned to donors at their request, others were donated to established college libraries at Connecticut College, Purdue University, Hunter College, Columbia's Teachers College, and most notably, several women's colleges, including Radcliffe, Barnard, and Smith.[37] Barnard and Smith continue to be known today for their strong commitment to documenting feminist activism.

Shortly after the collapse of the WCWA, the IAV became another casualty of the war. Although the initial fate of IAV was more definitive, in the end the archive's provenance would also prove more enduring. Shortly after the German invasion of Holland in May 1940, the IAV received two visits from German officials. By the end of June, the archive's founders had closed and sealed the institute.[38] Only months before the closure, in anticipation of the German invasion, Manus had moved her own personal papers and books to the IAV for safekeeping, which suggests that she considered the archive a highly secure site. Following the IAV invasion on June 12, 1940, at which time the German Security Police carted away all the contents of the organization from archival fonds and books to furniture and curtains, the IAV's founders began to investigate why the archive had in fact been seized.[39] Although they were initially told that the women of Berlin were interested in the IAV's materials, evidence suggests that no more than a small portion of the archives were ever accessed by German women.[40] The IAV, like so many other archives in Europe, was seized because it both promised to serve as a useful source of intelligence and posed a potential threat. In part, this assessment was based on the collection's link to Manus, a Jewish peace and disarmament activist, who was later questioned about her connection to the IAV and eventually captured (reportedly dying at either Auschwitz in 1942 or Ravensbrück in 1943).[41] The archive was also perceived as a threat because it was a hub of international activity. In her study on the IAV, historian Francisca de Haan concludes, "The Nazis did not confiscate the materials out of a primitive 'fear of women,' but because they saw the peace and other international activities of women such as Manus and the organizations she represented as dangerous and powerful."[42]

While Posthumus, the only surviving founding member of the IAV, initially spent several years attempting to recover the documents seized in 1940, over time she abandoned her search and focused on rebuilding the archive. Then, in 1992, only a few years after Posthumus's death, reports indicated that the seized IAV materials had resurfaced. Taken by the Red Army at the end of the war, the IAV materials were discovered in the Osobyi (Special) Archive in Moscow.[43] Haan concludes, "The content of the IAV, therefore, was not only relevant to women, but its political implications were realized by at least two governments."[44] Although it would take more than a decade, the IAV materials were eventually repatriated to Holland. Today, the IAV, now known as Aletta, Institute for Women's History, houses not only more than 85,000 books and brochures connected to the women's movement but also approximately 500 collections belonging to women and women's organization among other relevant materials and, after a nearly seventy-year absence, at least part of the IAV's original collection.[45]

If the story of the World Center for Women's Archives' rise and fall and the story of the International Archives for the Women's Movement's seizure by the Nazis and eventual resurfacing in post-Soviet Moscow are relevant to this study, it is not because they can necessarily be understood as points of origin for the feminist archives under consideration here but rather because these histories both point to the political efficacy of the "scrap heap" itself.

Like the archives and special collections to which I will turn my attention in subsequent chapters, the WCWA and IAV were established during a period of social, political, and economic struggle and heightened militarism,[46] as well as a period marked by a sharp decline in feminist activism. In the midst of these dramatic social, political, and economic changes, however, the world was also being restructured in other ways that share something in common with our own era. The 1930s was an era when new media technologies were shattering once taken for granted understandings and experiences of time and history. While the invention of the phonograph in the late nineteenth century had already opened the possibility of storing time, by the 1930s the rising popularity of radio was bringing about a much greater temporal shift: with radio broadcasting, events could unfold in real time. The effect on people's perceptions of time and history was, of course, profound. Time was becoming something that could be captured and stored; history was becoming something that could be witnessed in the making or quite literally in the present. In other words, the era's new media technologies enabled people to be in time and in history differently than they had been in the past. The 1990s and early years of the new millennium were similarly marked by profound changes in people's experiences of time and history. The internet and web have not only greatly expanded the possibility of real time communication and dramatically affected our ability to experience events without being physically present, but they have also deeply restructured our relationship to the past. Among other far-reaching impacts is the extent to which the internet has made archiving necessary and indeed unavoidable parts of everyday life. To write in a networked world, after all, is always already to be in the archive.[47]

The parallels between the WCWA and IAV and the archives and special collections that are the subject of this study, however, are not limited to the fact that these projects took shape during either periods when feminist activism appeared to be in decline (namely, the periods following the first and second wave feminist movements) and when our perceptions of time and history were being restructured by new media technologies. Indeed, the most remarkable similarities between the WCWA, IAV, and the archives and special collections that are the subject of this study are their shared mandates. The WCWA was committed to preserving documents and other materials related to the feminist movement and to serving as a site of education and mobilization for feminist work in the present. Moreover, although the WCWA was informed by Schwimmer's radical political orientation, which included a history of trade union organizing and feminist pacifist activism, the archive's structure and mandate permitted and even encouraged alliances with "the establishment." Indeed, from the onset a strong understanding maintained that alliances with money, power, celebrity, and established institutions, such as universities, would be necessary to realize the project. Finally, the WCWA recognized the role an archive might play in broader educational endeavors. Similarly, the IAV, however committed it was to collecting and preserving documents related to the women's movement, was also committed to participating in the production and dissemination of new materials related to the women's movement, a mission evidenced in endeavors such as the *Yearbook International Archives for the Women's Movements* (a multilingual annual that featured new essays on the women's movement, first appearing in 1937). The IAV also recognized the strategy and even necessity of being at least tangentially connected to existing institutions, such as the Netherlands Economic History Archive and International Institute of Social History.

If we take the WCWA and IAV as two points among others for the beginning of feminist archives, then it becomes apparent that feminist archives have long exceeded the desire to preserve historical gains. These histories foreground the extent to which feminist archives are produced out of a complex set of desires for preservation, education, and action. It is also significant, however, that both archives have had notable afterlives. The papers that remained after the collapse of the WCWA—the detritus of an archive—were dispersed to archives around the Northeast United States and subsequently laid the foundation for major feminist collections to develop at several colleges. As such, what mattered is not necessarily what the WCWA accomplished during its short, active lifespan but rather what its scrap heap subsequently yielded. Likewise, that the IAV would be seized and subsequently held as intelligence by two regimes during a nearly seventy-year period is also significant. The IAV's story reveals the archive's ability to intervene in political struggles across historical periods. Both archives also reveal that sometimes an archive's story may be as important as its contents. Ironically, then, both of these early attempts to establish feminist archives arguably proved most powerful and effective in their afterlives. And as I emphasize throughout this chapter and book, precisely this cycle of accumulation, collapse, dispersal, and redeployment remains central to the project of feminist archives today.

Archives with a "Focus on Women's Present"

Despite the fact that the World Center for Women's Archives was never fully realized, its contents and concept persisted, seeding collections at other institutions and informing the work of archivists and librarians decades later as the rise of the second wave feminist movement fueled new feminist archival projects. In Suzanne Hildenbrand's 1986 collection, *Women's Collections: Libraries, Archives, and Consciousness*, the WCWA is notably and continuously cited as a model for second wave feminist archives and special collections. In one essay, Hildenbrand, drawing a distinction between "traditional women's collections" and collections established in the 1970s to early 1980s, observes: "Traditional women's collections are concerned with women's past, but in recent years there has been a trend toward collections that focus on women's present."[48] One can only assume that Hildenbrand was not thinking of the WCWA when she refers to so-called "traditional women's collections" that focus more narrowly on women's history because, in many respects, the collections she describes as having a "focus on women's present" appear to share much in common with the WCWA's mandate. She writes:

> While traditional collections provide the sources for historical scholarship, representatives of the newer trend provide the documentation for social change. Even when research oriented, these collections support change in laws, hiring practices, admissions procedures and so on. Nurtured by a revitalized feminism they reflect the feminist agenda in their emphasis. . . . They may be held in university centers, non-profit organizations, or private homes. Many suffer from lack of funds, but others are generously

supported by grants. Some of these collections are marginal to the library world, others are leaders in it. No overview of women's collections today would be complete without an examination of representatives of this trend.[49]

Hildenbrand provides brief overviews of several exemplary collections in this category: university-based initiatives, such as the Center for the Study, Education and Advancement of Women at the University of California (Berkeley) and the Women's Educational Resources Centre housed at the Ontario Institute for Studies in Education (University of Toronto); externally funded nonprofit initiatives, such as the Catalyst Library and Audiovisual Center; organizational archives, such as the Marguerite Rawalt Resource Center of the Business and Professional Women's Foundation; and grassroots archives, such as the Lesbian Herstory Archives. That Hildenbrand could group such eclectic archives and special collections together may appear surprising. However, these collections shared in common *not* a single subject, context, or even political aim; rather than serve historians *per se*, these collections were established to simultaneously serve researchers of women's history and activists engaged in contemporary struggles. In this sense, these collections were as oriented to the past as they were to the present and future. What connected them were both their focus on women's and feminist issues and their particular orientation to time and history. To illustrate, I briefly turn my attention to two special collections established from the 1970s to 1980s.

In the mid 1980s, the Ontario Institute for Studies in Education's Women's Educational Resource Centre (WERC) was not only collecting materials related to the feminist movement but also serving as an information and referral center designed to "facilitate daily communication among women and women's groups."[50] Among other things, WERC provided access to "addresses and telephone numbers, project descriptions and announcements of meetings and other events" to women in the community.[51] The centre also produced educational materials, such as the "Women's Kit," which contained records, slides, pamphlets, and posters to assist with educational work beyond the institute's context.[52] In short, WERC was both a site of research that played a significant role in supporting the feminist and queer scholarship produced at the Ontario Institute for Studies in Education (OISE) in the 1980s to early 1990s as well as a community resource and meeting place for feminist activists and women seeking the services offered by feminist organizations. At WERC creating a space to collect historical documents, however, was *not* in and of itself considered a political act—the relevance of the collection was contingent on its ability to provide vital information to women in the present, especially frontline workers and grassroots activists.

By the time I started to regularly access WERC's resources in the mid 1990s, the center's original mandate was no longer apparent. With the decline of the second wave feminist movement and subsequent rise of the web, there was no longer a pressing need for an archive to also serve as a clearinghouse for mailing lists and phone numbers. In 1998, the books and printed matter once connected to WERC were officially acquisitioned by the OISE library, which had become part of the University of Toronto's larger library system. I encountered, therefore, the remains of a hub of feminist activism that I was well aware of but never experienced firsthand in an institution that was, by this time, already losing its well-established reputation as a major center of feminist scholarship. Yet, as longstanding WERC librarian Patricia Serafini suggests, the increased institutionalization of WERC was not entirely negative. Although it may have prompted the collection's drift away from its original mandate, it also enabled the collection to survive a period of cut-backs to libraries, archives, and feminist organizations. Serafini explains, "Once the collection moved to the [OISE] library, it actually received an acquisition budget which is generally $10,000 per year. Prior to this, books were donated and acquired on an *ad hoc* basis. Frieda [Forman] wrote to every organization that she knew of to solicit any documentation that was free of charge."[53]

While WERC continues to be significant to the extent that its modest budget enables the University of Toronto library system to acquire at least some feminist materials that may otherwise be overlooked, it no longer operates as a notable stand-alone collection. Indeed, its fate mirrors the fate of many feminist initiatives housed within universities where the founding principles of projects are so easily trumped by the struggle to survive in economically perilous times.

By contrast, the Lesbian Herstory Archives (LHA), which was originally housed in the home of Joan Nestle and Deborah Edel and to this day remains an entirely volunteer-run and donor-driven collection, has not only survived but also surpassed many university-based queer feminist collections in both size and significance. Despite its questionable approach into preservation (most professionally trained librarians and archivists recoil upon entering the LHA's basement where hundreds of printed documents, audio cassettes, vinyl records, and video recordings are housed in conditions that do not even come close to meeting the minimum standards of an "archival quality environment"), the LHA is arguably one of the most significant women's collections in North America today. Perhaps most notable is that if WERC and other university-based collections have adjusted their mandates over time to remain relevant within the institutions where they are housed or upon whom they rely for funding, the LHA's strident (and some might conclude even paranoid) relationship to established institutions and external funders has enabled it to not only survive but continue to grow during an era when other feminist and queer institutions have succumbed to neoliberalism's pressure to collapse or conform. On this level, the LHA's belief that "funding shall be sought from within the communities the Archives serves, rather than from outside sources" (an especially difficult mandate to uphold given lesbians' historically marginal economic position), while never making it a particularly well-endowed organization, has enabled it to remain at least somewhat protected from the cuts that have decimated so many other allied endeavors.

From its inception, the LHA has juggled various and eclectic goals. Beyond collecting the documents and artifacts of individual lesbians and lesbian organizations, the LHA is "a force for community building among lesbians, providing a welcome, and often a meal or lodging for visitors from out of town and actively networking among lesbians nationally."[54] Although the LHA is the largest and undoubtedly most important lesbian feminist collection in North America, if not the world, and hosts professional researchers on a regular basis (or as regularly as the archive's highly irregular hours of operation permit), its structure and mandate have changed little since its inception in 1974. Over the course of its long history, it has continued to combine private and public spaces. It is an archive with more than one sofa, a kitchen open to volunteers and visitors, and to this day a member of the collective lives in the house, albeit now in a separate apartment on the top floor.[55]

The first time I visited the LHA, I came as a poet rather than as a researcher. I was there to prepare for an event organized by the lesbian artist collective, Fierce Pussy, who had just launched an exhibit of their work at the LHA. When I arrived, I was greeted by a group of twenty-something-year-old volunteers who were, to my surprise, listening to a Ferron album released long before they were even born. As stated in the LHA's mandate, "archival skills shall be taught, one generation of Lesbians to another, breaking the elitism of traditional archives."[56] On the occasion of my first and subsequent visits, the presence of young volunteers, many born over two decades after the archive was conceived by Nestle and Edel, suggests that the LHA has managed to uphold this goal. This is an especially notable achievement because more than most surviving women's organizations from the 1970s, the LHA has clung to its original principles, many deeply inflected by the era's radical feminist and lesbian separatist ideologies. If it has managed to survive and attract the support of younger women, however, it is likely because the archive has not blindly clung to its original principles. Although it remains a community-based archive whose survival is contingent on sweat equity and small donations, it has made an effort to adapt to changing understandings of gender and sexuality (for example, by working to accommodate and accept the place of transgender women who identify as lesbians and transgender men who once identified as butch dykes).

As with my account of the WCWA, my interest in looking back at these archives with "a focus on the present" is not to privilege a single collection as more or less important in the history of feminist archives. I do think it is important to recognize, however, that at least in the 1980s when many university-based feminist collections, such as the ones located at Berkeley and OISE, were at their most active, their mandates were not distinctly different from the mandates and activities of community-based archives, such as the LHA. While their funding sources and connection to library and archive professionals may have differed, for at least a short time these collections were engaged in surprisingly analogous work as they attempted to create centers that would serve as sites of archivization, education, and community organizing. Moreover, there is little doubt that in the long run, the LHA's entirely volunteer-run collection has proven just as, if not more, enduring than many, if not most, of the institutionally-based feminist collections established in the 1970s and 1980s. Without drawing any definitive conclusions, the histories of second wave feminist collections, such as WERC and the LHA, especially when read against each other, are revealing. In short, they suggest that while institutional alliances, sustainable funding, and the oversight of professional librarians and archivists may be beneficial, they by no means guarantee a collection's long-term survival or relevance; by contrast, relying solely on the generosity, time, and gifts of community members is no guarantee that a collection's preservation will be necessarily compromised.

Such complex histories—histories that point to the possibility of radical political projects taking shape in established institutions, such as universities, and "institutions" taking shape and thriving despite antiestablishment politics and practices—are precisely those upon which the feminist archives and special collections at the center of this study continue to build. While conducting interviews for this book, however, I was especially struck by the number of professionally trained librarians and archivists who cite the LHA as an important predecessor to their more orderly institutionally-based collections. Even if their professional training makes them uncomfortable with some of the LHA's priorities and approaches to preservation, they embrace the LHA's belief that archives, history, activism, and community building can and should coexist. But this is not to imply that the collections at the center of this study are not unique on other levels. As explored in the following chapters, in contrast to earlier feminist collections, the collections featured in this study do not appear to be structured in relation to the apparent divisions between the community and academe or history and activism. While the women involved with university-based collections in the 1970s to 1980s felt compelled to defend their location inside the academy as well as their interest in history and archiving and felt compelled to temper their affiliations and interests by simultaneously serving as clearinghouses for information relevant to the current feminist movement, the archivists and librarians in this study do not necessarily consider their institutional affiliations at odds with broader political mandates. Indeed, they are unapologetically oriented to the past. Again, as I emphasize in the conclusion, their present is deeply historical. What has changed over the past century is not necessarily a recognition of what an archive or collection can do—in many respects, the collections in this study simply extend work that has been ongoing in different ways at least since the 1930s—but rather what a "focus on women's present" might mean. And in this present, feminism's scrap heap has become irreparably linked to feminism's future.

Political Failure, Temporal Drag, and Feminist Nostalgia

About the time that many women born since 1968 started to collect the seemingly ephemeral traces of our cultural activism but before, I assume, any of us anticipated the possibility that we would soon establish collections of just such debris in archives across North America, Lauren Berlant published an article reflecting on her ambivalent relationship to radical pasts. "'68, or Something" appeared in *Critical Inquiry* in 1994. The article begins with Berlant's personal account of being dismissed as "so '68." The accusation was launched after Berlant collectively authored, with a group of feminist colleagues, a memo to the other members of the Committee on Critical Practice, an interdisciplinary group of scholars at the University of Chicago. The memo in question began by boldly stating, "For us the main disappointment of CCP [Committee on Critical Practice] has come in its failure to inhabit a space of concrete utopian imagining."[57] This alone, Berlant concludes, was enough to incite the scathing response that she and her colleagues were, quite simply, "so '68." As Berlant observes, for her colleagues, '68 had not only become synonymous with political failure; it was also "a bar to reimagining a radical relation of politics and professional life."[58] To be accused of being "so '68" was tantamount to being accused of imagining and more critically daring to articulate some other way of being in the world and the academy long after such bold endeavors could be reasonably proposed. After all, 1992 was a moment when it appeared as if the only forms of resistance that could exist were those that took the form of minor, barely visible gestures (walking through the city, poaching texts, reading against the grain). To be properly in *that* moment was to be on the side of tactics not strategies, ambivalence not doctrine, subjectivity not collectivity, and certainly *not* community or anything else remotely pointing to the possibility of a mass movement. Most important, "'68, or Something" was written "in favor of refusing to learn the lessons of history, of refusing to relinquish utopian practice, of refusing the apparently inevitable movement from tragedy to farce that has marked so much of the analysis of social movements generated post '68."[59] It was written with the intent of placing "'68 in a scene of collaborations and aspirations for thinking, describing, and theorizing social change in a present tense, but a present tense different from what we can now imagine for pragmatic, possible, or useful politics."[60]

Reading Berlant's article more than fifteen years later, I am struck by the extent to which the article—a defense of attaching oneself to a failed political moment—represented not only a great political risk at the time of its publication (an arguably more skeptical and cynical era) but also one conversation among many that would cultivate a growing interest in time, history, and political failure among queer feminist theorists over the coming decade. Her project here, after all, is not only to question how "political breakdowns work as something other than a blot, or a botched job" but also to take seriously how past political moments might be used to understand social change in the present—a present not quite yet obtainable. If I raise Berlant's article here at all, I do so in part because it reminds us that to be so '68 in '92 or '94 was much worse than being so '74 in '09 or so '80 in '11 and so on. The questions, then, are simple: what exactly has changed? And to what extent is this shift integral to understanding the archival turn in contemporary feminism?

At issue for Berlant is a single but by no means easily resolvable dilemma. In short, she asks us to consider how an attachment to a failed social revolution might be reconceived as a political strategy. Embedded in her challenge is not only a project that entails a radical rethinking of failure, especially political failure, but also one that demands a rethinking of both time and history outside the lens of capitalism, patriarchy, and compulsory heterosexuality. I would like to suggest that among other things that have changed since the early to mid 1990s when Berlant published her article is the turn to time and history in queer theory and politics and perhaps, more explicitly for queer feminists, an unabashed interest in understanding the past as an essential, generative, and complex scene of contemporary political struggle. The possibility opened up by Berlant and by other theorists of queer time is a possibility that not only offers to unfetter us from the constraints of temporal logics (for example, to be in time against the expectations of the institutions that govern most of our lives, including all the typical arms of the Institutional State Apparatus) but also to develop a relationship to history that is neither simply teleological nor naively comparative. Indeed, "in a queer time and place," one might be present in the past, or be already past the present, or anticipate a more hopeful future by retreating to the past. This is precisely the appeal of Freeman's notion of "temporal drag" cited earlier in this chapter. In fact, one might even read Freeman's notion of temporal drag as a viable response to Berlant's much earlier call to consider how political breakdowns may be understood as something other than "a blot, or a botched job."[61]

No longer assuming that intergenerational conflict and "anxiety of influence" are givens, Freeman's notion of "temporal drag" works on the assumption that even if and when the past feels like a bit of a drag, quite literally, it may also be a site of hope and political renewal. While Freeman's theorizing on temporal drag did not appear for more than a decade after Berlant's article calling for a radical rethinking of political failure, she emphasizes that "feminist temporal drag itself had already emerged in the early to mid-1990s as a self-reflexive tactic of personal style, of performance, and of collective identification among young women who flaunted nonhegemonic femininities in misogynist urban hardcore scenes."[62] As Freeman explains, the "girl-sign" at the center of Riot Grrrl always already "acknowledged an uncontrollable past, the uncontrollability of the past, its inability to explain the present."[63] To the extent that the girl-sign opened up the possibility of an uncontrollable past and emphasized that the past cannot always already be understood simply as that which precedes the present, it also changed how a younger generation of feminists understood time, history, and subsequently the role and possibility of archives.

On the one hand, this chapter has emphasized the extent to which the archival turn in contemporary feminism is part of a legacy of feminist archiving. Long before any of the collections featured in this study were conceived, feminist archives and special collections already existed in communities and on university campuses across North America. To understand the archives discussed in the following chapters outside this history would be to misrepresent the conditions under which they have accordingly taken form. On the other hand, there is also no doubt that the conditions under which earlier feminist archives were established no longer exists. If women such as Rosika Schwimmer and Rosa Manus still needed to persuade other women and men of the need to preserve women's documents and more specifically traces of the feminist movement, and if many second wave feminists felt compelled to justify the relevance of expressing their politics through a commitment to archiving and history, then today feminist archives require neither explanation nor justification. If touching the past once felt impossible for feminists or conversely at odds with more immediate political concerns, for women born during and after the rise of the second wave feminist movement both touching history and being engaged in its making have become part and parcel of what it means to be an engaged feminist activist, cultural worker, or scholar in the present. Indeed, understanding that one never can know for certain when one is really past something and further appreciating that the scrap heap may be as much a source of parody and pleasure as it is a location from which to strategize on present and future political interventions, feminists born since the late 1960s are in time and history differently. And as explored at length in chapter 2, being in time and history differently is integral to fostering not only new forms of political alliances, including those that appear to defy temporal constraints, but also new narratives about feminist history and feminist futures.

2 / Archival Regeneration: The Zine Collections at the Sallie Bingham Center

When does a generation begin and another one end when we are describing communities of practice?

—CLARE HEMMINGS, *Why Stories Matter*

If the feminist archives featured in this study are unique in the history of feminist archival initiatives, then it is to the extent that they represent a relationship to time and history that has only recently become possible. After all, these archives reflect the sort of relationship to time and history that one can only experience *after* one is both certain that they have a history (perhaps, only after one begins to feel the weight of such a history and at least some responsibility for its preservation) and certain that history itself is ultimately fleeting—something never entirely sheltered from the whims of the present. At stake here is an understanding of history as something that may be as vital as it is elusive, daunting as it is malleable, and a recognition of time as something deeply nonteleological and antiprescriptive— something that, like space, might just as easily be occupied as passively received as a force that simply wears against the body. As a result, much more is at stake here, too.

As Clare Hemmings argues in *Why Stories Matter*, feminists have consistently constructed feminism as "a series of interlocking narratives of progress, loss, and return that oversimplify [its] complex history."[1] Along the way, different politics have calcified around different eras, making it impossible to grasp "the possibility of feminist spaces of friendship, desire, affiliation, and productivity that produce variegated historical accounts whose subjects (of any age) shuttle back and forth between their own and others' memories, representations, and fantasies of past, present, and future."[2] The archive stories that follow in this chapter demonstrate how contemporary feminist archives hold the potential to place pressure on these narratives, especially the generational narratives that continue to structure so many popular accounts of feminism. The archive stories recounted here more specifically highlight the potential for archives to foster productive political alliances across seemingly distinct generations and eras and to promote new narratives about feminist politics and thought while simultaneously opening up the possibility for political interventions to be realized (or realized again) long after their initial appearance. At stake is the potential for a politics deeply attentive to history but by no means bound by the temporal logics that continue to structure and limit understandings and experiences of feminism in the present.

In the following discussion, I not only recount stories about my encounters with specific texts and collections housed in the David M. Rubenstein Rare Book, Manuscript, and Special Collections Library at Duke University but also reflect upon how these encounters were both informed by and led to a reevaluation of my earlier research. Specifically, I consider how my research in the archives at Duke offered an occasion to return to my research on feminist zines, which I initiated in the mid 1990s. As a result, I caution that the archive stories that follow are told from multiple temporal standpoints and exhibit little regard for the linear passage of time. Like the archive, they are informed and structured by unanticipated proximities and by the connections such unanticipated proximities foster.

Back to Bitch

On my second visit to Duke University in early 2011, I did precisely what I did on the occasion of my first visit five years earlier—I asked to see the boxes that comprise the Sarah Dyer

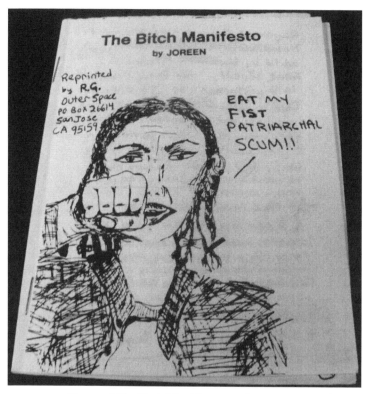

FIGURE 2.1. Cover of *The Bitch Manifesto* zine featuring image by Laura H (Sarah Dyer Collection, Sallie Bingham Center for Women's History and Culture), courtesy of Liz Henry.

Collection, a collection of more than 2000 zines donated by Dyer, the founder of Action Girl Comics. In sharp contrast to my usual way of operating in archives (an often meandering methodology based on the assumed epistemological value of the researcher's inevitable drift from texts to bodies to contexts), this time, my intent was to start with Box 1 and methodically work my way through the collection over the course of a four-day visit. As it turned out, my most significant finding appeared only an hour into my research. Somewhere between *13* and *Crumpy*, I discovered *The Bitch Manifesto*—the zine version, that is.

By coincidence, I had already rediscovered "The Bitch Mani-festo" a few months earlier when my colleague, feminist activ-ist and scholar Ann Snitow, presented me with a copy of *Notes from the Second Year*, where Joreen Freeman's manifesto was originally published in 1970.[3] Although I was already familiar with Freeman's manifesto when I received the copy of *Notes from the Second Year*, I now found myself reading the manifesto in its original context for the first time, including the striking opening line—"BITCH is an organization which does not yet exist"—and resonate conclusion, "The organization does not yet exist and perhaps it never can."[4] Emphasizing that BITCH does not yet exist and may never be fully realized, Freeman locates BITCH firmly in the future. In other words, BITCH appears as a refusal of the here and now, a potentiality, a desire for a possible world. From start to finish, BITCH, like so many aspects of radi-cal feminism, is a utopian gesture.

Of course, reading Freeman's words more than forty years after the manifesto's original publication, I was *already* in the future, albeit not the one imagined by either Freeman or most radical feminists. Rather than transport me into the future, a possible world that has not yet arrived—a world that was, at least for a brief moment in the late 1960s to early 1970s, something a young feminist activist might dare to imagine and articulate—rediscovering "The Bitch Manifesto" in its original context brought me back to a present I never had the opportunity to experience in the first place. But because I recognize that BITCH, like so many radical feminist propositions, remains unrealized, rediscovering the manifesto also served as a reminder that evocative calls from the past can circulate as more than nostal-gic refrains. Here, in the "future," encountering the projected world of a past political moment may create the grounds for unanticipated alliances, collective enterprises, and collabora-tive projects that bring together fellow travelers from different generations and even different times. In other words, for women born after 1970, reading something like "The Bitch Manifesto" in 2011 or 1992 or 2017 might do more than educate them about the past. Such moments also offer readers an opportunity to tap into some of the energy and rage that motivated Freeman and her coconspirators in the early years of the second wave feminist movement to imagine a different world. This is precisely why *The Bitch Manifesto*—the zine version, that is—is relevant to this discussion.

Although many zines in the Sarah Dyer Collection borrow titles from earlier feminist concepts and slogans (for example, *Blue Stocking* and *Not Your Bitch*), *The Bitch Manifesto* is more than a provocative title—it is a verbatim reprint of Freeman's original manifesto. There is nothing particularly unusual about the fact that the manifesto is reprinted because most zines feature materials pilfered from other texts, including first and second wave feminist publications and ephemera. There are, however, at least two things that distinguish *The Bitch Manifesto* from most other zines. First, Freeman's manifesto does not reappear in the zine version as a pastiche but is reproduced in its entirety. Second, in contrast to most zines, which reproduce texts with little or no regard for copyright, the zine producer, identified only as "Lizzard Amazon" from "Riot Grrrlz Outer Space," provides detailed bibliographical information, informing her readers that "The Bitch Manifesto" is by "Joreen" (or Jo Freeman) and originally appeared in *Notes from the Second Year* in 1970. Most surprising, however, is the fact that Lizzard Amazon goes one step further by issuing an apologia not only to Freeman but also to the publication's editors, Shulamith Firestone and Anne Koedt. The handwritten note on the zine's inside front cover simply reads: "Dear Jo, Shulamith and Anne I hope y'all are not offended that I'm reprinting this w/out permission. I just want girls today to see it!"[5]

A few months earlier, my own rediscovery of "The Bitch Manifesto" had prompted me to think more seriously about the possibility of unanticipated alliances that stretch across eras, prying open opportunities for collaboration between social actors past and present. And, perhaps, this is why I felt compelled to photograph Lizzard Amazon's note to Freeman, Firestone, and Koedt, upload the photo to my computer, and email it—directly from the archive—to Ann Snitow, who, I knew, had been in dialogue with all three intended recipients at some point. My email was not intended to serve as a direct act of transmission but merely a shared observation, as in "Interesting, look where the dialogue continued..." To my surprise, however, when Ann emailed back the following day, she mentioned, "In the same batch of emails with yours was one from Jo Freeman about the Republican assault on abortion. She is the great, relentless 'bitch' she always was!"

For at least a year after this coincidence, I knew exactly what happened next—naturally, Ann forwarded my photograph of Lizzard Amazon's note to Freeman. Indeed, I was so convinced that this *was* what happened that I wrote about the serendipitous turn of events in an earlier version of this chapter. But if BITCH is the future—a future that may never arrive—so too is this archive story. Based on a series of encounters with texts and people, some real and some apparently imagined, the serendipitous turn never happened. As I was completing this chapter nearly a year later, I approached my colleague just to confirm that I had in fact got the story right. While Ann recalled receiving my email, she assured me that she never forwarded the message to Freeman or any of the other intended recipients—*that* part of the story I had imagined. This is the point where most researchers would shelve the story—after all, why admit to falling prey to one's imagination? Rather than shelve this archive story, however, I want to consider some of the questions the story raises. Recognizing that my story was the result of a proximity opened up by the archive, what is the relationship between archival proximity and our own desires? Said another way, what is the relationship between the past and potentialities, between history and possible worlds?

Whether the message, written from one feminist activist to several others across the decades, ever reached its intended addressees is incidental here. In this archive story what matters is not the delivery of the message but rather the extent to which the archive produced new and potentially productive proximities between social agents rarely imagined occupying the same space and time. If Lizzard Amazon of Riot Grrrlz Outer Space (notably, it is "Riot Grrrlz Outer Space"—a location with no definable coordinates) was unable to directly communicate with Freeman and the editors of *Notes from the Second Year* when her zine first appeared (presumably in the mid to late 1990s), by the time her zine entered the archive, her proximity to these feminist trailblazers had already shifted.[6] After all, Lizzard Amazon's reprint of the "Bitch Manifesto" and *Notes from the Second Year* carry more or less the same status in Duke University's David M. Rubenstein Rare Book & Manuscript Library. On the most technical level, in this context they are both individual publications that are part of larger donated collections. In addition, in the archive, the chance that Lizzard Amazon's message might finally be read by one of her intended recipients or by someone with a direct connection to them increases. In contrast to the original audience, primarily other zine producers (in this case, mostly younger women engaged in feminist politics and cultural production in the 1990s), in the archive, a publication's audience may expand well beyond that originally imagined. In this archive story what matters most is not that the archive created a real or fully *realized* dialogue across the generations but rather that the archive produced a space to imagine an encounter that otherwise may have remained unimaginable. As I emphasize throughout this chapter, archival proximity is about the uncanny ability to occupy different temporalities and to occupy temporalities differently, thereby collapsing the rigidly defined generational and historical logics that continue to be used to make sense of feminist politics and theory.

The Zine Collections of the Sallie Bingham Center

The Bitch Manifesto, as previously noted, was one of the 2050 zines donated to Duke University's David M. Rubenstein Rare Book, Manuscript and Special Collections Library by Sarah Dyer in 2000. Dyer's decision to donate her zines to Duke University was initially prompted by a flood in her home but finalized only after careful consideration of the established reputation and collecting mandate of the Sallie Bingham Center for Women's History and Culture,[7] an endowed research institute housed in the university's rare book and manuscript library. In "A Brief History of My Life in Zines," an essay commissioned by the Sallie Bingham Center, Dyer candidly explains, "We had a flood in our basement. Thankfully, the zines were stored in an area that wasn't touched, but a lot of our things were water-damaged and I decided that if I really wanted to see these zines preserved, I needed to find a safer place for them."[8] In late 1999, she sent off "a blind 'hey, do you think you might want this stuff I have' email" to Duke University. After an affirmative response and a few exchanges, she felt confident that her zines would be respected, preserved, and "serve some useful purpose," and as a result, she started to ship them box by box to Duke University from her home on Staten Island.[9] But why send her collection to Duke University's Sallie Bingham Center rather than any number of suitable collections in the New York City area? Duke University is not only geographically distant from Dyer's home but at the time of her initial donation, the center had not yet acquired a reputation for collecting materials related to the contemporary feminist movement. In fact, the archive's reputation for collecting contemporary feminist materials largely followed Dyer's donation.

Dyer emphasizes that her decision to donate her zines to Duke University was based on two major factors. First, she recognized that the zines in her collection—highly personal, fragile, and hand-bound documents made by girls and women—shared much in common at the level of content and form with the other materials found in the collections at the Sallie Bingham Center. In an interview carried out for this book, Dyer elaborated, "As many of the zines are one-of-a-kind and certainly many of them are delicate, I was mainly concerned with finding an archive that had extensive experience with that sort of thing."[10] She further explained that because "there was an emphasis on ephemera and one of a kind items like diaries" within the collections at the Sallie Bingham Center, she felt assured that the archivists "would know what to do" with her zines.[11] As such, for Dyer, the archive's experience working with particular types of documents (for example, personal papers and one-of-kind books, including artist books) influenced her decision. Second, Dyer was interested in placing the collection of zines in an archive with a focus on women's history. Dyer's recognition that her personal collections of zines responded to the Sallie Bingham Center's established collecting mandate, however, is somewhat surprising. On the one hand, the center has a mandate to collect materials related to "women of color," "women's sexuality and gender expression" and "girl culture," and to collect materials related to women's literature, art, scholarship, and feminist activism. On the other hand, the center has a mandate to collect the materials of "Southern women," "domestic culture," and so-called "church women."[12] In short, the center's collecting mandate, while not inherently conservative, reflects a wide range of local and national interests and appears to be rooted in stable and even essentialist notions of gender identity and women's experience that have more often been challenged than embraced within Riot Grrrl or third wave feminist discourses. However, for Dyer, the collection's focus on historical materials and books and documents connected to earlier forms of girl culture (for example, girls' literature from the early twentieth century) ultimately proved more important than the archive's affiliation with any specific feminist ideology.[13] On the basis of Dyer's professed interest in earlier forms of girl culture, Kelly Wooten, the archivist who oversees the Sarah Dyer Collection and other zine collections housed at the Sallie Bingham Center, has come to affectionately and respectfully refer to Dyer as her "deputy librarian." As Wooten explains, "Sarah also collects girls' literature and has donated some of it, which we catalog separately. I call her my 'deputy librarian,' since she has such a good collecting sense in general."[14]

Notwithstanding Wooten's deep appreciation for Dyer as a discerning collector of not only contemporary feminist materials but also other materials related to the history of girls and women, Dyer is surprisingly self-effacing about her status as a collector. When asked if there was a particular moment when she realized that she was archiving not only zines but also in many respects a particular moment in the feminist movement, Dyer told me, "Truthfully, it was always an accumulation rather than a collection—I didn't seek out any of the zines except for the handful I had ordered before I started the *Action Girl Newsletter*. After that, it was all comprised of zines submitted for review. And I kept everything!"[15] Although she confesses that at some point she did realize "something big was happening" because "the range of zines was staggering and seemed important in some way," the realization only reinforced her decision to keep everything.[16] Her realization did not significantly change either what she chose to keep or the conditions under which she stored the materials she was accumulating in her home. Moreover, despite the fact that Dyer eventually recognized the potential research value of her zine collection, she did not anticipate its immediate impact on contemporary scholarship:

> I had no idea how, or even if, the zines would be used after I donated them. Before I contacted the Sallie Bingham Center I saw some of the research projects that were being done on their other collections, so I knew that it was possible. And I certainly hoped that future researchers, or even just readers, would find them of as much value as I did. But I think I was expecting something more along the lines of the research being done on, say, pioneer diaries. I expected that years from now someone would come across the collection and think "how interesting!" I didn't realize that they would be put to use right away![17]

Despite Dyer's own assumption that the value of her collection would be realized only in the future, the Sarah Dyer Collection had an immediate impact. In 1999 when Dyer first contacted to the Sallie Bingham Center, Riot Grrrl and third wave feminist materials were only beginning to migrate from personal collections to public and university archives. Indeed, with the exception of an initial donation of zines by Tristan Taormino to the Sophia Smith Collection at Smith College the same year, at that time, researchers seeking to carry out research on Riot Grrrl or third wave feminisms were still primarily working with private stashes of documents or in haphazard community archives and libraries, such as Seattle's Zine Archive and Publishing Project (ZAPP) or the Olympia Zine Library.[18] While such collections are by no means insignificant, they are neither equipped for long-term preservation of fragile documents nor supported by the resources to catalog large collections of zines in a manner that makes them easily accessible to researchers. Dyer emphasizes this point: "The thing that the archives achieve," she maintains, "is that they assemble and organize the zines, making sure that researchers get an idea of the vast breadth of the medium. I think it would be very difficult to get a true picture of the world of girl zines by trying to order or find them yourself."[19] Because Dyer's collection encompassed some of the earliest materials related to Riot Grrrl and third wave feminism to be acquired by an established archive and because it represents an especially large individual collection (18 boxes and 18.3 linear feet),[20] its presence at Duke University impacted not only the reputation of the Sallie Bingham Center, resulting in several subsequent donations of zines and contemporary feminist documents, but also the type of research being carried out at the center.

When I first met Kelly Wooten in 2006, she had just begun her full-time position at Duke University. Nevertheless, she was already familiar with the collections she was now charged with overseeing. Wooten had volunteered at the center prior to being hired full-time, and she had even written a thesis on the Sarah Dyer Collection while completing her graduate studies in library science.[21] By the time I met her in 2006, the Sarah Dyer Collection was already gaining a reputation as an important repository of documents on Riot Grrrl and other forms of contemporary feminist activism and cultural production. As Wooten explained at the time, since acquiring Dyer's collection in 2000, several other private collectors, mostly women in their late twenties to mid thirties, had contacted the archive about potential donations. The biographical notes and collection overviews provide insight into what I have come to read as a pattern of collecting integral to feminist knowledge and cultural production and activism in the 1990s and beyond. In the finding aid for the Amy Mariaskin Zine Collection, for example, we learn that Mariaskin, the author of two zines, "began collecting and trading zines with other women as a member of the Pittsburgh, PA, Riot Grrrl Chapter from 1995 to 2002."[22] Although her collection is much smaller in scale than Dyer's collection, its scope is similar:

> Collection consists of about 150 zines, mostly self-published by women and girls in the United States. Subjects include feminism, riot grrrl, body image and consciousness, music, mental health, depression and mental illness, film, poetry, rock and punk music, comics, violence against women, sexual identity, homosexuality and bisexuality, transgender issues, and race.[23]

The finding aid for the Sarah Wood Zine Collection, which consists of approximately 150 zines, explains that Wood, along with her friend Kelly Curry, "founded and owned GERLL Press (Girls Empowered Resisting Labels and Limits), a zine distro [distribution service] based in Chicago, Ill., in the early to mid 1990s."[24] Their collection includes zines "submitted to Wood and Curry by their authors to be considered for sale through the distro" on the subjects of feminism, the Riot Grrrl movement, body image and consciousness, women's health, women athletes, sexual abuse, television and film, poetry and short stories, rock music and punk music, violence against women, sexual identity, homosexuality, and bisexuality.[25] On the occasion of my second visit to Duke University in early 2011, Wooten told me that she had since received donations from even younger women, including Sarah Maitland who first visited Duke University as a zine researcher.[26] Like Dyer, Mariaskin, and Wood, Maitland had a history of involvement in the production and distribution of zines by girls and women and had had the foresight to collect the zines of other girls and women. In this respect, all four donors carry similar profiles as cultural producers with a keen sense of awareness of why it may be important to house self-published works by young women in an established archive. Albeit for different reasons, these women also appear to recognize that locating their zine collections within an archive with other collections of documents related to the history of girls and women and/or more specifically, first and second wave feminist publications and manuscripts is essential to historically contextualize the writings of a new generation of women. In short, they understand the recontextualization of their collections as a form of *authorization by association*.[27]

The arrival of the Sarah Dyer Collection at Duke University, however, resulted in more than subsequent donations from younger feminist cultural producers and activists. As Wooten observes, "The purpose is to be collecting for the future, but we know that people are using these materials in the present."[28] Since the arrival of the Sarah Dyer Collection in 2000, the collections housed in the Sallie Bingham Center have increasingly been accessed by researchers engaged in contemporary scholarship. The list of recipients for the library's Mary Lily Research Grant, which provides scholars with travel awards to visit collections housed in the Sallie Bingham Center, for example, reveals that since 2005, there has been a steady increase in the number of researchers visiting the center to carry out research on zines, Riot Grrrl, and third wave feminisms.[29] One of the first recipients to visit the center with the intent of carrying out research on Riot Grrrl and third wave feminisms was Alison Piepmeier, the author of *Girl Zines: Making Media, Doing Feminism*. Drawing on Piepmeier's study and my own earlier research on girl zines,[30] among other studies, I consider how the migration of feminist zines from private collections to established collections of women's and feminist documents informs new perspectives on the materiality and content of girl zines. Specifically, I reflect upon how my visits to the zine collections at Duke University in 2006 and 2011 prompted me to reconsider conclusions drawn in my own earlier research. Although girl zines are by no means the primary subject of this book or even this chapter, they are the reason I found myself visiting collections of contemporary feminist documents in the first place, and they are therefore part of the prehistory of this book.

Mapping Continuities

If the publication of Piepmeier's 2009 study, *Girl Zines*, was significant, it is by no means because it offered insight into a cultural phenomena that had not yet been theorized. Since the mid 1990s, dozens of articles and books have been published on the subject, both by curious readers/researchers of zines and by former zinesters turned commentators and scholars.[31] In many respects, the vast number of publications on the subject is not surprising. More than most "subcultural" phenomena, girl zines, especially those that appeared in the early days of Riot Grrrl, were always already in dialogue with the theories that would eventually be used to make sense of them as cultural objects and discourse. As Piepmeier observes, "The idea of zines as sites of theory production may be somewhat surprising, as theory is generally associated with elitist academic practices, and zines occupy the opposite end of the spectrum."[32] However, as she further notes, it is precisely the tension between theory and abstraction and "the intensively and intentionally local, individualized, and eccentric" where "third wave theory is produced."[33]

Although Piepmeier correctly observes that girl zines are unique to the extent that they frequently appear to be the result of a productive tension between engagements with scholarly discourses and popular culture and subcultural practices, in contrast to earlier studies on zines (my own work included), her study steers clear of the tendency to posit girl zines as necessarily unique cultural objects. Indeed, in contrast to previously published studies, which typically gloss over the link between zines and earlier grassroots feminist media traditions (for example, the volunteer-produced newspapers, magazines, and even perfect-bound books published by radical feminist collectives throughout the 1970s and 1980s), Piepmeier's study is marked by a deep attentiveness to girl zines as an *extension* of established traditions of media making in feminist communities. Thus, although Piepmeier continues to map out a history of feminism as one marked by the surge and recession of distinct "waves," the story she presents about girl zines and by extension feminism since the 1990s actively troubles the assumption that Riot Grrrl and third wave feminism and their cultural manifestations necessarily marked a radical break with earlier forms of feminist thought, cultural production, and activism. In a chapter focusing on the "feminist legacy of grrrl zine," for example, Piepmeier maintains:

> Rather than being aberrations, in my origin story grrrl zines are actually part of a significant trend in women's history . . . women throughout the nineteenth and twentieth centuries have created informal publications—from scrapbooks to women's health brochures to mimeographed feminist pamphlets—and a textual and formal analysis of these publications suggests that they are the direct historical predecessors of grrrl zines. . . . Positioning grrrl zines within this feminist history makes women's continued resistance visible and enables us to begin creating a more accurate picture, not only of zines but of third wave feminism. I contend that the third wave, like the grrrl zines that helped initiate it, is part of feminist history and not a unique break from the past. An exploration of grrrl zines shows that the rhetoric and iconography of the third wave are distinct from earlier feminist generations, but many of the underlying impulses propelling this feminism are similar among all the waves of feminism.[34]

Girl Zines does not contain a metanarrative on the collections in which Piepmeier carried out her research, but, as I discovered in the course of my own research, much of her research was carried out at Duke University and other collections featured in this study, including the Barnard Zine Library (discussed at length in chapter 4). While I cannot say for certain that Piepmeier's analysis was directly informed by the fact that her research was carried out in the context of collections housing feminist documents from earlier periods, it is worth noting that her perspective is shared by many of the feminist archivists and librarians I encountered over the course of researching this book, including Wooten. In fact, if I noticed any difference in Wooten's understanding of the zine collections at the Sallie Bingham Center between the occasion of our first interview in 2006 and our second interview in 2011, it is the extent to which she had developed a deeper appreciation for the zines as part of a legacy of grassroots feminist media production. In our 2011 interview, for example, she explained, "Although some of the third wave published materials have a 'this is not my mother's feminism' attitude, I've talked to many feminist activists about this issue, and many of the well known third wave women have worked closely with second wave feminists—they are not rejecting second wave feminism because they have learned from that generation of women."[35] Wooten followed this comment by drawing my attention to several specific zines that highlight the overlaps and dialogues between second and third wave feminisms. For Wooten, that the zine collections at Duke University are especially well positioned to highlight the lines of continuity across different eras of feminist publishing, politics, and thought is precisely what distinguishes the collection from other collections of feminist zines, including those at Barnard College and those housed in community-based archives. After all, as part of the Sallie Bingham Center, which has a mandate to acquire, preserve, and make available "published and unpublished materials that reflect the public and private lives of women, past and present,"[36] the zines are brought into proximity with everything from women's diaries and letters from the late nineteenth century to meeting minutes and newspapers produced by second wave feminist collectives.

The stock and trade of feminist publishing has long been in documents that can be produced quickly, inexpensively, and, most notable, without vetting from outside publishers or the potential censorship imposed by commercial printers.[37] In short feminist publications have favored accessibility over durability, resulting in a legacy of highly ephemeral documents. As Wooten emphasizes, regardless of the era, most feminist publications have been made "with materials at hand."[38] For example, "Most of the second wave women's movement publications were made on a mimeograph. The text is typed or handwritten. Whatever they could print with was the means of production."[39] In *Girl Zines*, Piepmeier confers, noting that the mimeograph was so important to the second wave feminist movement that an advertisement for the 1996 Feminist Expo proclaimed, "the current wave of the feminist movement began with mimeograph machines."[40] Yet, by the early 1990s, the mimeograph had been all but replaced by the copy machine, and second wave feminist newsletters, pamphlets, and broadsides were giving way to a younger generation's zines. The means of production and products, however, were analogous. In both cases, the privileged mode of production enabled texts to be produced quickly, inexpensively, and independently, and both were marked by a distinctive quality (or lack of quality) underscoring the urgency of the messages being communicated. For example, a survey of second wave feminist newspapers and magazines reveals that the quality of writing, including the number of typos (intentional and unintentional), rivals the quality of writing found in many zines. Often collectively produced and produced under conditions where volunteers, including those with no previous experience in publishing, played a major role, both second wave feminist and Riot Grrrl and third wave feminist publications are marked by notable inconsistencies in style and design. This, however, is also indicative of "participatory media." Defining "participatory media" as "spaces in which individuals become creators rather than simply consumers of culture," Piepmeier emphasizes that from the scrapbooks kept by first wave feminists, which offered women a means to archive their engagements in public life, to second wave feminist newsletters and newspapers to zines, participatory media has long played a central role in feminist organizing.[41] On this basis, she further maintains that girl zines from the 1990s and early years of the new millennium may be best understood as part of a "*continuum of feminist participatory media*" (emphasis my own) and can thereby be used to chart how Riot Grrrl and third wave feminisms, far from representing a rupture with earlier feminist discourses, extended them in what many people perceived to be a "post-feminist" era.[42] This is also where my own research story comes into focus.

In my earlier research on girl zines, initiated in 1994, I erroneously read dialogues with second wave feminism primarily as parodies of an earlier generation's politics, aesthetics, and sensibilities. Admittedly, at the time I was too deeply immersed in poststructuralist feminism to appreciate that behind these playful parodies, the zines I was writing about were deeply influenced by and even invested in a previous generation's feminist discourses, even those simultaneously being dismissed as irrecoverably essentialist. As research for this book brought me back to the subject of my earlier research, I found myself returning to many of the same zines but through a different theoretical and political lens and in a radically different context—this time, in the archives and special collections which now held so many of the zines discussed in my earlier research. From this new vantage point and context, texts and images I had read as parodies of second wave feminism in the mid 1990s now appeared endearingly attached to earlier feminist texts, icons, practices, and slogans. In some cases, they even appeared deeply nostalgic for another place and time in the history of feminist politics, thought, and activism. To illustrate, I turn my attention to *Out of the Vortex*, writer Sarah Marcus's early publication.

In 1995, when I first encountered Marcus's writing, the author of *Girls to the Front: The True Story of the Riot Grrrl Revolution*, was a seventeen-year-old high school senior living with her parents in a suburb of Washington, DC. At the time, I had just started graduate school, was living with a girl in an all-girl band, and questioning the political efficacy of my scholarly pursuits. At some point, I decided to expand a short paper on Riot Grrrl zines into a thesis length project, and I sent away for more than one hundred girl zines—one of the zines and letters that arrived was from Marcus. *Out of the Vortex* stood out for its carefully edited, even journalistic writing, as well as meticulous layout (for example, without ignoring the signature markers of zines, which include pasted-up fragments of typewritten and handwritten text, *Out of the Vortex* was surprisingly legible and orderly, even featuring conventions such as page numbers). My reason for inviting Marcus to be a research participant, however, had less to do with her zine's legibility and more to do with the fact that even in 1995, Marcus was already an insightful commentator on Riot Grrrl and contemporary feminism. In the seventh issue of *Out of the Vortex*, published in 1995, for example, Marcus published an article titled, "Zine Theory." Here, she outlines why zines are important as political tools in the present:

> I've been thinking a lot lately about zines, especially but not exclusively girl zines, as political tools. The 1970's battle cry "the personal is political" means to me that our experiences are not isolated. Everything that happens to us is connected. . . . Only by controlling the medium do we control the message. We are the medium; we are the message. For this reason zines are extraordinarily unique and powerful political tools.[43]

In her "zine theory," Marcus notably refers to the "1970's battle cry 'the personal is political.'" The gesture is twofold. On the one hand, by referring to "the personal is political" as "the 1970's battle cry," Marcus establishes a strategic distance from a feminist ideology she associates with another place and time. On the other hand, she uses the citation as a way to support her own position that "everything that a person feels a personal need to put into a zine is valid."[44] That Marcus both distances herself

from and embraces second wave feminism is by no means surprising. After all, as Marcus explains in the introduction to *Girls
to the Front*, her exposure to second wave feminist publications
and institutions is precisely what enabled her to find the Riot
Grrrls in the first place. Like most people, Marcus discovered
Riot Grrrl only after reading the 1992 *Newsweek* article, "Revolution, Grrrl Style." Determined to find the subjects featured in the
article, Marcus started to scour local newspapers for advertise-
ments listing Riot Grrrl meetings. Then, she explains:

> In early 1993, I finally found an address for the DC chap-
> ter of Riot Grrrl. It was printed in *off our backs*, a long-run-
> ning feminist journal I had discovered during my weekend
> sojourns at the feminist bookstore. The women of the *oob*
> collective were publishing like it was 1973, doing their lay-
> out by hand and printing on flimsy newsprint. But one of
> them interviewed a few riot grrrls—and listed the group's
> post office box address.[45]

Ironically, for Marcus, direct access to Riot Grrrl came via two
important second wave institutions. She located contact information in a copy of *off our backs*, a collectively run feminist
newspaper founded in 1970, and she found the copy of *off our
backs* in one of the only places that would carry such a publication—a feminist bookstore.

When I reencountered *Out of the Vortex* for the first time
in nearly a decade while I was carrying out research at Duke
University, Marcus's interest in and debt to second wave feminism, which I overlooked in my earlier research, was suddenly
apparent. Between the various commentaries by Marcus and
her coeditor and guest contributors about dating, parents, and
punk, there are commentaries that point to a temporal orientation that is deeply attentive but by no means nostalgic for the
past. In one article, for example, Marcus performs a close reading of *The Underground Guide to Colleges*—an alternative college guide published in the 1970s. Based on the guide's conde-
scending insights into "how 'liberated' the chicks on the campus

are," which she observes appears to be targeting male readers interested in knowing how likely their female classmates will be to "put out," she concludes, "This book only further convinced me of the abject sexism of the hippie counterculture to which some kids today seem to eager to return. You can't be a feminist and a hippie; it's that simple."[46] Again, Marcus's commentary pushes the 1970s back—into its proper place—as an era when women often remained in highly subjugated roles despite the broader social transformations underway, but at the same time Marcus's commentary also reaches out to the era's women by recognizing their struggle and explicitly acknowledging that sexual liberation was not inherently liberating for women. Her reading is surprisingly nuanced and most notably empathetic. A few pages later, just before a series of reviews on other Riot Grrrl and feminist zines, such as *I'm so Fucking Beautiful* and *The Nerdy Grrrl Revolution*, Marcus's coeditor, Joan, reviews *Our Bodies, Ourselves*, which like *off our backs*, was first published in 1970 by a feminist collective. As if the book had just appeared for the first time, Joan enthuses, "I wonder where I would be without this book. I don't want to sound phony, but this book is such a well-written resource on women's health that I urge everyone to get their hands on a copy."[47] Why doesn't Joan "want to sound phony"? Does she fear that her enthusiastic review will sound disingenuous because it is too enthusiastic or because she is reviewing a book originally published twenty-five year earlier, long before she was born?

In my visit to the zine collections at the Sallie Bingham Center, *Out of the Vortex* was not the only Riot Grrrl zine where the dialogue with second wave feminism was newly apparent to me. In *Hungry Girl Fanzine*, I discovered a reprint of Marge Piercy's "Barbie Doll," originally published in the 1973 collection, *To Be of Use*.[48] *Living Hell Lady* cites a quotation by Kate Millet, "Sex is a political category," as part of a pastiche of images and texts, including an advertisement for the controversial contraceptive option, Depo-Provera.[49] In *Function 5*, quotations by Simone de Beauvoir and Betty Friedan bookend a reprint of Judy Syfer's ironic essay, "Why I Want a Wife."[50] *Don't be a Pussy* includes both an address for Naiad Press, a lesbian press founded in 1973, and an appeal to readers to write away for their catalog because "they sell lots of cool books."[51] A copy of *Femcore* includes a reprinted photograph from an Equal Rights Amendment rally and excerpt from the ERA decision passed in 1972.[52] Beyond the ideological similarities, like their elders at *off our backs*, whom Marcus observes were still "publishing like it was 1973" in 1993, girl zines from the 1990s and beyond also frequently feature clip art synonymous with early feminist publications, including the ubiquitous women's symbol and women's power symbol. Wooten speculates, "Who knows? Maybe their mom had a stash of second wave feminist publications in the basement and that was their source? Either way, it's obvious that zinesters in the 1990s, a pre-internet era, were clipping images and in some cases, texts out of second wave feminist publications."[53]

Although there is much to say about the continuities between second wave feminist publications and Riot Grrrl and third wave feminist zines, my concern is with the extent to which the migration of girl zines into the archive has rendered these continuities increasingly visible and with the more important implications of this migration for future research on feminist zines and more generally feminism. As Piepemier maintains, girl zines are important because they were "a site for the development of late-twentieth-century feminism."[54] Following Piepmeier, I argue that at stake in the recontextualization of girl zines—a process carried out in part through their relocation in established collections of women's and more explicitly, feminist documents—is how placing this key "site" for the development of feminism since the early 1990s in relation to early feminist documents might alter narratives about feminism's past, present, and future. Here, then, the archival turn in contemporary feminism emerges as an integral part of not only an essential way of understanding and imagining other ways to live in the present, as I emphasize in the introduction to this book, but also potentially a way to respond to Clare Hemmings's urgent call to discover new ways to tell stories about feminism's past, present, and future.

Telling Other Stories about Feminism

As Hemmings argues, Western feminism has, to its detriment, relied on narratives of progress, loss, and return to make sense of its history. Among other problems, embedded in these narratives are deeply entrenched assumptions about intergenerational dynamics. In "loss narratives," a previous generation waxes nostalgic about the "good old days" of feminist activism when the future of feminism was still bright. In "progress narratives," feminist elders are routinely cast aside as misguided or misled, overly utopian, essentialist, and even racist, while a younger and more politically and theoretical astute generation surfaces as the *only* political agents capable of understanding the complexity of the contemporary political terrain—here, old and young hold nothing in common. In "return narratives," feminist generations unite to move forward into the future, but as Hemmings observes, "what must be relinquished—epistemological and ontologically—remains generationally distinct."[55] Like my critique of Susan Faludi's thesis of "feminist matricide" in chapter 1, Hemmings draws attention to how the "generational logic" underpinning accounts of contemporary feminism is both heteronormative and homosocial, as they assume that women's crossgenerational relationships are always already hostile.[56] Such narratives further privilege time over context, rarely acknowledging specificity of place as a factor in the development of feminist politics, thought, and expression.[57] Most notable, however, generational narratives both entrench the idea that we are in a postfeminist era and more problematically ascribe the blame to one generation or another: "If feminism has been lost, or if it remains as anachronism, then this is always someone else's fault."[58] If a considerable effort has been made "to retain the temporality of Western feminist storytelling as generational," Hemmings maintains that it is due to the desire to uphold the "empirical inaccuracy of what is represented."[59] In short, the temporal investments of contemporary feminist thought bolster claims that "some other generation" is responsible for feminism failing to fulfill its promise—a promise that is itself apparently deeply inflected by different generationally defined desires. The assumption, of course, is that different generations, wherever one draws the line, desire different things from and for feminism, but this too is a fiction. After all, as Hemmings asks, "When does a generation begin and another one end when we are describing communities of practice?"[60] But if generation, like gender or race, is understood as a social construct rather than a naturalized form of difference, this is not necessarily a question whose answer can be taken for granted.

As suggested throughout this chapter, the archive is a key site where these problematic generational logics can be loosened and are already beginning to come undone. I would like to suggest that the work of undoing generational logics operates on at least two axis in the archive. First, there is substantial evidence that attempts to challenge the generational logics underpinning contemporary accounts of feminism that often begin in the archive. This most obviously happens when younger feminists are quite literally brought into contact with the documentary traces of earlier generations' of feminists. Hemmings recounts this phenomenon in the introduction to *Why Stories Matter*:

> I still remember my surprise when I first visited a feminist archive, perused newsletters and magazines from activist groups, and realized that discussions about sadomasochism in the lesbian community had been raging long before the "sex wars" and that black feminist and transnational critiques had been a consistent component of feminist theory, rather than one initiated in the late 1970s or 1980s. For me, that moment of realization not only emphasized the importance of personal experience, luck if you like, in one's relationship to history, but also precipitated an ongoing discussion in my head about the best way to respond to absences from contemporary accounts.[61]

As suggested in the above account, for Hemmings, being in proximity to an earlier generation's conflicts and contradictions was a turning point in her own thinking about feminism. Here, proximity unsettled her assumptions about feminism, prompting her to question the extent to which she had internalized the "truth" of deeply oversimplified accounts of feminist thought and activism. In similar ways, my previous account of rediscovering some of the zines I had written about in the mid 1990s reminds us that the archive is a context that fosters new interpretations. But in contrast to Hemmings, in my case, the archive offered a context in which to reinterpret my own generation's history in relation to a much longer history of feminist thought and activism.

As emphasized in the first archive story presented in this chapter, the archive holds the potential to produce much more than new readings of existing feminist debates. Beyond prying open previously obscured perspectives, it holds the potential to unmoor subjects from the historical moments in which they have become calcified. Indeed, as I suggest in my account of the *Bitch Manifesto*, it may produce the conditions for dialogues between different generations of feminists and even the possibility for alliances that defy generational and temporal logics. Yet the archive also holds the potential to authorize and legitimize voices that may otherwise remain unheard, opening up the possibility for voices that arrived "before their time" to be heard and for other voices to remain audible long after their assumed time. In this respect, my research echoes Janice Radway's ongoing study on girl zines and the broader textual communities and networks they fostered in the 1990s and beyond. As she emphasizes, zines have complex afterlives lived out in a range of different sites and modes: "Zines themselves live on in transmuted social contexts—in archives and circulating collections, in classrooms, on Web sites, and in the writings of former zinesters, zine fans, and zine analysts. As a consequence, zines continue to exert their effects through the activities of their altered former creators and through those of the new readers they engage."[62]

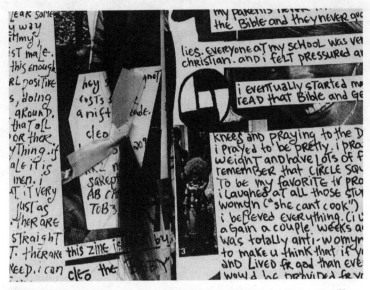

FIGURE 2.2. Locket of hair in copy of *Slut Magnet # 8* (private collection of author). Photo taken by author.

Integral to their complex afterlives is the fact that although they initially circulated as texts that primarily supported what Hemmings aptly describes as "progress narratives," apparently affirming a break in feminist politics and thought with the coming of age of women born during and after the rise of the second wave feminist movement, in the archive, they no longer necessarily serve to support such narratives and in fact function along an entirely different axis. The "afterlives" of zines, facilitated in part by their migration to archives and special collections, have enabled them to reintervene in the construction of narratives about feminist politics and thought. But the "afterlives" fostered by the archive are not limited to fostering political alliances and forms of interpretative interference that defy temporal logics. As the concluding archive story in this chapter reveals, these "afterlives" are also about the uncanny ability of subjects to remain social agents outside their designated time.

Cleo's Hair

To be clear, Cleo's hair was not something I encountered in the archive. But this should not come as a surprise. Organic materials, such as hair, pose a threat to the integrity of documents. In many archives, the body, even the researcher's hands, are constructed as a threat. What I encountered in the David M. Rubenstein Rare Book, Special Collections and Manuscripts Library at Duke University was not Cleo's hair, but rather its predictable absence. Nevertheless, Cleo's hair is part of the prehistory that haunts this book.

I encountered Cleo's hair long before anyone imagined that girl zines, such as Cleo's *Slut Magnet,* would ever find their way into an archive. The hair in question was discovered in the form of a thick lock ironically tied together with a piece of purple ribbon and slipped between the pages of *Slut Magnet #8.* Although "Cleo," not her real name, offered no explanation for the inclusion of the hair (presumably her own), the content of the zine provided insight into the unusual insertion's possibly intended signifying effects. Like most issues of *Slut Magnet* (published from 1994 to 1995 and circulated primarily to other zine producers within an extensive textual network of girls), the body is invariably present as a subject if not as a tangible artifact. Beyond the recurring commentaries on body image, especially concerning the pressures placed on young women to adhere to feminine social norms, the corporeality of the zine producers' everyday rituals from throwing up to slashing to masturbation are described in detail. *Slut Magnet* might be read as an account of extreme self-fashioning where remaking the self is expressed (and enacted) not only through repeated self-affirmations but also through graphic retellings of ritualized forms of self-abuse and body modification. From the confessions and rants that appear in the zine, it is possible to recover at least a partial portrait of the writer. At the time the zine was written, Cleo was in her mid-teens, living in a small town in a conservative and Christian household, and struggling to come out as a lesbian, albeit only to herself and other girls in the textual community she had established through the exchange of zines and letters. Given the writer's tenuous position, it is little surprise that she continuously writes about her body as a site of both shame and pleasure and empowerment. *Slut Magnet #8* begins with a confession about an earlier self-perception of her body: "I prayed to be pretty. I prayed to lose weight and have a lot of friends."[63] As she wryly observes, "I was into compulsive praying and look where it got me?"[64] Having transcended the naivete of both religion and the compulsion to reproduce normative notions of gender and sexuality, Cleo goes on to describe and enact how she is actively working to reclaim her body. The zine is replete with affirmations that highlight the writer's new attitude toward her body: "You can call me fat and ugly as much as you want because I can look in the mirror and see that im beautiful."[65] However, these affirmations are interspersed with graphic retellings of her attempt to violently remake her body: "I have ten xacto blades in my room on my windowsill and every fuckin one has ripped against my flesh."[66]

This is not the first time I have written about Cleo's lock of hair. Its discovery was a particular poignant moment for me as a researcher. A gesture obviously wrought with symbolism, one might read it as an attempt to insert the body, quite literally, into the text. In a text already deeply focused on the body and bodily traumas, the desire to insert part of the body into the text might even point to the writer's recognition of language's limited capacity to represent the corporeal. Hair, of course, is also deeply connected to the abject and to specific affects, most notably disgust. Hair is both of and not of the body. It is both alive and dead. A liminal material, the signifying effects of hair are complex and contradictory. My concern here, however, is not with the liminality of hair but rather with the liminality of the archive itself and the possibilities pried open at this threshold. On the occasion of my first visit to Duke's David M. Rubenstein Rare Book, Special Collections and Manuscripts Library, when I asked to see the box containing the zines beginning with "S," it was not *Slut Magnet* but rather the lock of hair I wished to reencounter. More than a decade later, I still wondered whether the lock of hair was intended for me in particular or was simply one lock of hair among many that appeared in the eighth issue of *Slut Magnet*. The lock of hair mattered because of the questions it continued to raise about both the status of the zine in question and my own more general relationship to this particular zine producer. At this threshold, I was presented with a chance to return to these questions that I had not quite yet answered.

In my earlier research Cleo's hair stood out as an especially notable moment to the extent that the hair, a liminal artifact, forced me to think more seriously about the presence of bodies in the textual community at the center of my research. In this new context—a rare book library—the presence of the zine itself now held a similar effect. Like the lock of hair, which I initially received reluctantly as a somewhat too intimate and too abject gift tucked between the pages of a zine, in a rare book library far away from its place of origin, the presence of the zine, with all its personal confessions, also felt somewhat too personal. The encounter, however, foregrounded for me the extent to which the girl zines I had been carting around for more than a decade had, unbeknownst to me, already established a very public afterlife. While I know nothing about what actually happened to Cleo, or more precisely the young woman behind the persona known as Cleo, it was evident that she had already been regenerated in the archive. But if the archive holds the potential to regenerate subjects on some level, was Cleo's time the early to mid 1990s when her zine was in circulation or rather now or even in the future? After all, in the archive, she is evidently no longer struggling to establish a community where she can speak and be heard. By virtue of her place in the archive, she has arguably already arrived somewhere. In the archive, Cleo's previous attempt to make herself anew through her zine becomes, in a sense, a completed project. Now her liberated, open, irreverent persona can thrive without outside interference. In the archive, there are neither parents censoring the mail nor dismal nights spent contemplating X-Acto blades on window ledges. As a researcher who has long worried about whether this particular research participant survived, the archive provided at least some assurance that Cleo, if not the young woman who fabricated this persona, eventually found a safe home, one where she will continue to be encountered and reinvented by future generations of readers. Here, in the archive, I am more or less assured that Cleo not only survived her adolescence but will also remain completely fixed in its time and place. Paradoxically, then, the archive opens up the possibility of survival and stasis, longevity and temporal dislocation, reminding us again that the archives under investigation here are unique in their ability to bring generations together and to keep subjects in time differently.

3 / Redefining a Movement: The Riot Grrrl Collection at Fales Library and Special Collections

The Riot Grrrl Collection is about the future—thinking ahead to the status of materials in one hundred years.

—LISA DARMS, senior archivist,
Fales Library and Special Collections

In the early 1990s , most people in North America, including most feminists, had never heard the term "Riot Grrrl." By 1993, Riot Grrrl was synonymous with a style and politic signifying a new feminism—a feminism for the "video-age generation . . . sexy, assertive and loud."[1] This is the story told by Sara Marcus in *Girls to the Front.* Like most people, Marcus discovered Riot Grrrl in the November 23, 1992, issue of *Newsweek.* As Marcus emphasizes in the history of Riot Grrrl she would publish nearly two decades later, for the young women connected to the Riot Grrrl scene in Olympia, the autumn of 1992 had been marked by a series of attempts to thwart the mainstream media's cooptation of their growing movement. The *Newsweek* article was "a culmination of the madness that had been going on all fall. The big difference was that the girls had managed to beat back all the previous incursions, but this time the media got its story."[2] The consequences of the *Newsweek* article and subsequent mainstream media profiles on Riot Grrrl were widespread. On the one hand, the article served as a call to arms for younger girls, like Marcus, who were not already connected to the Riot Grrrl scenes in Olympia, Washington DC, and Minneapolis. On the other hand, the *Newsweek* article opened the media floodgates, placing Riot Grrrls on the defensive in an economy of representation they had previously subverted through their astute suspicion of the mainstream media and savvy deployment of DIY media. Although it would be misleading to imply that Riot Grrrl necessarily lost control of its image after the *Newsweek* article, the publication of "Revolution, Grrrl Style" represented a turning point—Riot Grrrl had gone viral.[3]

In many respects, the announcement of the Riot Grrrl Collection at Fales Library bore uncanny resemblance to the movement's initial "discovery" by the mainstream media. Lisa Darms, senior archivist at Fales Library and Special Collections, explains that news of the collection's development was never a secret, but its announcement was also not something that remained entirely in either her control or that of the collection's donors:

> We issued an internal newsletter, which is for the library. It's not private, but it's simply a print and pdf newsletter about acquisitions. It generally goes to alumni and donors. They wanted to announce the acquisition of Kathleen Hanna's papers. It was amazing to watch how quickly—I think the next day—at the *L Magazine*, someone who was probably associated with NYU in some way, found it and scanned it in black and white and put it on their online magazine. From there, it went viral. At that point, I barred myself—I worried about a flurry of people contacting me because it hadn't gone through the press office, which is the normal way we would do such things, but instead of anyone contacting me, all subsequent articles referred back to that one *L Magazine* article. I was somewhat ambivalent about it. I wasn't trying to keep the collection secret, but I did want to reach a certain number of potential donors before making it public.[4]

However, neither Darms nor her donors, including Kathleen Hanna and Becca Albee who were preparing their papers at the time of the announcement, are strangers to the media's viral potential. In 1992, all three women were students at Evergreen State College in Olympia, Washington, where they witnessed and to varying degrees were implicated by the initial media capture of Riot Grrrl. If anything, the conditions under which news of the collection's development went public were all too familiar.

Although the *L Magazine*'s decision to scan and repost an article about the development of the Riot Grrrl Collection from an internal university newsletter and its subsequent impact is far less significant than the historical arrival of Riot Grrrl in the mainstream media, the similarities are worth considering.[5] Like Riot Grrrl in its early stages of development, which was both public and fiercely protective of its ability to control its representation and circulation,[6] the development of the collection was by no means a secret, but from the onset there was an attentiveness to maintaining control over the collection's publicity. As Darms explains, the desire to control the collection's representation was partly rooted in a commitment to ensuring it would not be defined too narrowly: "I don't want it to be the 'Kathleen Hanna Collection.' She feels the same way. It's a Riot Grrrl Collection, but most of the press was just about Kathleen."[7] Darms was also concerned about mitigating the circulation of misinformation about who would be able to access the collection and under what circumstances.

In the days following the *L Magazine* post, news of Fales Library's Riot Grrrl Collection traveled quickly over multiple forms of media, proving especially viral in forms of media that had not yet come into being when Riot Grrrl entered most people's consciousness in 1992 (for example, blogs, Twitter and Facebook).[8] If many archivists and special collections librarians spend years attempting to generate interest in their collections, for Darms, this achievement was effortless. That news of an archival collection could "go viral" reveals as much about Riot Grrrl as a cultural phenomenon as it does about the significance of the Riot Grrrl Collection. The media interest in the collection points not only to what is potentially controversial about the collection's development but also to the collection's status within a network of women, which includes women old enough to have heard Bikini Kill play live in the early 1990s and young enough to have been born after the *Newsweek* article, who identify with Riot Grrrl as an aesthetic, cultural, and political movement unique to their generation of feminists. My primary concern, however, is with neither the controversy nor the affective attachments generated by the collection. As I explore throughout this chapter, preservation *is* a central part of the Riot Grrrl Collection's mandate, but the collection holds the potential to do much more than preserve Riot Grrrl as it has been understood to date. As the collection develops, it also holds the potential to impact Riot Grrrl's legacy and more specifically the legacies of the women most closely identified with its development. As I argue, the Riot Grrrl Collection may thereby be read as a radical form of "position taking" enacted in and through the archive.

Pierre Bourdieu's theorizing on the field of cultural production offers a useful framework for beginning to understand how the creative products of a so-called "subculture" might be transformed through their entry into the archive and more specifically, how archivization might hold the potential to *retroactively* align previously unconsecrated cultural works with avant-garde movements. As Bourdieu maintains, every literary or artistic field is a *"field of forces"* and *"field of struggles,"* and the meaning of a work changes with "each change in the field within which it is situated for the spectator or reader."[9] The task of the literary or art critic is to understand the space of positions and "position-takings" within the field of cultural production. This, however, is an invariably difficult task because the critic must reconstruct all the people, forces, and conditions that shape the field at any given time. On this basis, Bourdieu emphasizes that any sociology of art or literature must be able to account for "the social conditions of the production of artists, art critics, dealers, patrons, etc."[10] and "the social conditions of the production of a set of objects socially constituted as works of art, i.e. the conditions of production of the field of social agents (e.g., museums, galleries, academics, etc.) which help to define and produce the value of works of art."[11] The objective is ultimately to understand any work of art or literature as a "manifestation of the field as a whole, in which all the powers of the field, and all the determinisms inherent in its structure and functioning, are concentrated."[12]

Bourdieu's theorizing aptly draws attention to the extent to which literature and art are symbolic objects constituted by the institutions through which cultural products are endowed with value. While he lists many of the most obvious institutions engaged in such work, including museums, galleries, and the academy, he does not list the archive. Because there is no doubt that the archive does belong in this list, the oversight is especially notable, but the archive is also uniquely situated in the field of cultural production. Unlike either the gallery or art museum, which usually endows a literary or artistic work with value in the present, the archive's work is more often than not retroactive. In other words, the archive is uniquely located to the extent that it permits works to migrate across the field of cultural production at different points in history. In this respect, a work originally produced primarily for a mass audience (or a work perceived as such) might become aligned with a work produced as "art for art's sake."[13] The archive, thus, is not only an institution that Bourdieu overlooks in his theorizing on the field of cultural production but also the institution that arguably holds the greatest potential to disrupt the field as it is conceived in his work. Once more, as I emphasize, this is especially relevant to questions concerning the designation of an "avant-garde."

While Bourdieu's "field of cultural production" evidently privileges the spatial, his theorizing on the avant-garde is first and foremost temporal. If "conservatives" recognize their contemporaries in the past, then the avant-garde has no contemporaries and "therefore no audience, except in the future" (107). An avant-garde, according to Bourdieu, establishes itself not by recognizing their contemporaries in the past but conversely by pushing "back into the past the consecrated producers with whom they are compared" (107). If Bourdieu's theorizing on cultural production fails to account for the question of the archive, then perhaps it is because the archive, more than any other institution, holds the potential to interrupt this supposed process by prying open opportunities for an avant-garde to be established retroactively. This is not surprising, however, because the archive is first and foremost a temporal apparatus—at once committed to the endless accumulation of time, as Foucault emphasizes in his theorizing on heterotopias,[14] of which library or archive exist as one example among many, as well as to the reordering of time. As I emphasized in chapter 2, materials in the archive are not necessarily aligned according to temporal logics. Players once estranged in the field of cultural production may become aligned. Contemporaries may be torn apart. Movements may be defined or redefined. In short, archival time challenges Bourdieu's assumption that avant-garde movements are necessarily established via a series of displacements—through the anachronization of one's predecessors. In the archive, an avant-garde conversely may be established via a series of strategic realignments that *make present* players who never had the opportunity to play in the same field but in many respects comfortably occupy the same field nevertheless.

The archive as an apparatus can be effectively wielded in a reparative manner, and this is precisely the movement I chart in this chapter. I specifically examine how relocating the Riot Grrrl papers from haphazard personal storage situations across the United States to the Fales Library and Special Collections in New York represents an attempt to redefine Riot Grrrl as a cultural movement as deeply marked by feminist politics and punk aesthetics as it is by legacies of avant-garde art, performance, and literature. After all, in contrast to the other collections featured in this book, the Riot Grrrl Collection is housed in an archive known for its art and culture collections (for example, the Avant-Garde Collection and the Downtown Collection) rather than holdings related to women's history. As a result, across Fales Library's special collections, one discovers the papers and cultural artifacts of several generations of innovative visual artists, performance artists, and writers. Among them are many figures cited as influences on Riot Grrrl.[15] The difference between the Riot Grrrl Collection at Fales Library and existing collections of Riot Grrrl related materials at Barnard College and Duke University, then, exists in not only the types of materials these collections house (the papers and artifacts of individuals versus documents always already intended for public or semi-public circulation, such as zines) but also the histories these collections hold the potential to advance. Thus, while preservation remains the central goal of the Riot Grrrl Collection, the collection also serves other purposes: most notably to legitimize materials that may otherwise slip into historical oblivion and to authorize them as *cultural* rather than exclusively *subcultural* products and more significantly to validate the materials as cultural products with a particular lineage in an urban twentieth-century North American artistic and literary avant-garde.

Archive Viral

Past attempts to develop archival collections dedicated to women and the women's movement have met considerable resistance. By comparison, the development of the Riot Grrrl Collection solicited little criticism. Nevertheless, the first response to the announcement on the *L Magazine* website read, "At what point does this become ridiculous?"[16] Reactions to the provocation were uniformly critical of the writer's implied accusation that the Riot Grrrl papers do not merit archivization. As the first response asked, "Why look down your nose at this? It seems perfectly reasonable to me that this stuff would wind up in a library. You can't study feminism in 2010 (or 2005 or 1995, for that matter) and not talk about Hanna and the Riot Grrrl movement."[17] Subsequent responses on the *L Magazine* website and other blogs reiterated the fact that the collection is one of historical significance. For example, two weeks after the *L Magazine* announcement, the following blog post appeared on *Jukebox Heroines*:

> I have been trying to get copies of Kathleen Hanna's, as well as, other Riot Grrrls zines from eBay and such, with

some success. I mean, since they were photocopied, you can make more, but after a while, the copies of copies of copies get rather hard to read. I am so happy that Riot Grrrl and the movement is getting some credit from the academic side. I mean they have for a bit, some texts have been written about it, but preserving these documents ensures it will never be forgotten![18]

Like earlier responses on the *L Magazine* website, Emily's post emphasizes the historical significance of Riot Grrrl. Her post also suggests that, despite the fact that a zine, for example, may continue to be copied and even sold on eBay for an indefinite period of time, there *is* an integrity to the original and that "originals" may be important, even in movements where appropriation and copying are integral and celebrated practices.

Defenses of the Riot Grrrl Collection's relevance were by no means limited to those rooted in making a case for the historical significance of the materials in their original form. In the days following the media leak, affective attachments to the papers being processed at Fales Library also came to the surface. Another participant in the spontaneous debate on the *L Magazine* website replied, "I applaud the NYU Library for taking the feminist movement and the *L Magazine* theory seriously, and am thrilled to see such a crucial part of *my* history, and countless others, illuminated by critical thought and inquiry. Not because we need the academy to validate who are ... but because it's an historical moment in time worth knowing about" (emphasis my own).[19] Feelings of personal attachment are also expressed in Macy Halford's op-ed piece published as part of "The Book Bench" column in *The New Yorker*:

I'm extremely happy that the papers of Kathleen Hanna—Riot Grrrl, Bikini Killer, Le Tigress—are going to the growing Riot Grrrl archive at N.Y.U.'s Fales Library. Happy because I live in New York and I might be able to think up a reason to gain access (I'm not in the academy, but would that stop any self-respecting grrrl?), and happier because it represents a major step toward overcoming the sticky formulation

Girl = Dumb, Girl = Bad, Girl = Weak

as Hanna and her sisters put it in the Riot Grrrl Manifesto, first published in 1991 in "Bikini Kill Zine 2."[20]

Halford assumes that the Riot Grrrl Collection will become a destination for researchers and fans and thus serve as Riot Grrrl's equivalent to, let's say, Graceland. This assumption is shared by Alyx Vesey. In a post about the collection on *Feminist Music Geek*, Vesey enthused, "it's with great excitement that I report that Kathleen Hanna is donating her personal papers to NYU's Fales Library for their Riot Grrrl Collection (which I didn't know they had) . . . Looks like *this moi* has got some independent research to do. See you in the stacks."[21]

While these comments represent only a few of the hundreds of responses posted online in the wake of the Riot Grrrl Collection's announcement, they are representative of the public reaction to news of the collection's development. First, despite the critique expressed in the initial response to the *L Magazine* article, the collection solicited few questions about whose history and what types of history count. The absence of negative responses to the collection's development suggests not only that Riot Grrrl's legacy may already be well recognized (at least in some contexts) but also that both inside and outside the academy there is a growing recognition that histories of minorities, activist movements, and subcultures are histories worth preserving. The initial response to the Riot Grrrl Collection also revealed that it is by no means a typical archival collection (despite its similarities to existing collections at Fales Library).[22] In contrast to most collections, for example, the papers and artifacts in question belong to not only living writers, performers, and artists but also women writers, performers, and artists who are, for all extensive purposes, still early in their careers.[23] In addition, it is significant that the excitement about the papers' arrival in the archive was shared by academic researchers, fans and people with political affinities to Riot Grrrl. This is not to suggest, however, that the researcher, fan, and affinity group member are by any means mutually exclusive categories. In fact, both responses to news of the collection's development and the content of the collection, which provides further evidence of Riot Grrrl's intellectual roots, reveal how deeply entangled these categories can be and arguably always were in Riot Grrrl. Finally, the dialogue generated by news of the collection's development revealed the extent to which the collection, despite its location in an institutional setting, is part of the affective economy in which souvenirs, memorabilia, and archival objects circulate. As Ann Cvetkovich reminds us, "memories can cohere around objects in unpredictable ways."[24] In other words, an object's meaning and value are invariably prone to drift, frequently becoming invested with attachments previously unimagined by the original producer or owner. Although these are the papers of individuals, news of the collection was received with enthusiasm because so many women feel that these papers represent and belong to an entire generation of feminists. This very identification enabled the Riot Grrrl Collection to go viral before its contents were processed, but this identification or overidentification with Riot Grrrl and specifically with key figures may be what the collection's development ultimately quells.

Although it seems likely that news of the Riot Grrrl Collection traveled as quickly as it did because many women feel a personal attachment to the materials the collection does now or will eventually house, the collection is defined by and asserts a much more narrowly conceived understanding of Riot Grrrl than existing collections of Riot Grrrl related materials. If existing collections, such as the zine collections at Barnard College and Duke University, have sought to promote an understanding of Riot Grrrl as a mass movement of girls and young women that originated in the 1990s, the Fales Library collection defines Riot Grrrl as a somewhat more temporally, if not geographically, bound movement synonymous with the cultural contributions of a core group of women musicians, writers, performers, and visual artists.

First, the Riot Grrrl Collection at Fales Library spans a specific period—1989 to 1996—although the dates are, as Darms acknowledges, "not 100% firm."[25] When asked about the temporal bounds of the collection, Darms explains that in many respects, 1989 represents "the intellectual inception" of Riot Grrrl,[26] because, by this time, Hanna and many other women connected to early Riot Grrrl activities were already at Evergreen State College and beginning to engage in the conversations that would lay the foundation for the movement. Although some materials in the collection, such as those related to Hanna's second band, Le Tigre, postdate 1996, Darms suggests that by 1996 both Bikini Kill and the Riot Grrrl movement were already in decline. Situating the collection between 1989 and 1996 is not necessarily inaccurate, but it does entrench the idea of Riot Grrrl as a cultural phenomenon that happened in a particular place and time and involved a specific group of individuals. As a result, rather than the "every girl's a riot girl" mantra that informs collecting policies at other institutions, one might conclude that the Fales Library's Riot Grrrl Collection is more explicitly engaged in and committed to canon formation, albeit not without a healthy dose of self-reflexivity about the trouble of canons.

Despite this mandate, which may strike some fans as being at odds with Riot Grrrl's ethos, it is important to recognize that the collection's existence is contingent on longstanding friendships and connections that date back to Riot Grrrl's inception in the early 1990s. As previously mentioned, Darms was a student at Evergreen State College in the early 1990s. "I never went to a Riot Grrrl meeting," she explains, "But I was there and involved and doing the same things. . . . I wasn't close friends with all the donors, but mostly, we were at least in the same places, at the same shows, at the same parties."[27] Perhaps more important, however, is Darms's present connection to the women she first met at Olympia in the early 1990s. As emphasized, the widespread interest in the collection has been generated in part by the personal attachment so many women feel to the collection's materials. The collection arguably only exists, however, because the donors and archivists identify with and trust each other on the basis of their much less public history. Nevertheless, when I asked Darms about the importance of her personal connection to the donors, she initially hesitated to admit to its centrality in the collection's development:

KE: It seems to me that this collection would simply not exist if you weren't friends or at least acquaintances with many of the donors.

LD: I'm not sure. Maybe it wouldn't exist at this time. Marvin Taylor, the Director of the Downtown Collection, is excited about the materials and had some knowledge of them . . . but no, you're right, the collection wouldn't exist yet.[28]

Later in the interview, Darms admitted, "I personally don't have a problem with my personal relationship to my donors, but I'm concerned and keep waiting for someone else to have a problem with it."[29] When asked to elaborate, she added: "Although a lot of curators and archivists probably have a personal relationship to their donors and that is pretty standard, I still worry. There is no money exchanging hands and there is nothing that benefits me personally, so I'm not sure why I'm worried."[30] I wondered whether Darms was concerned about finding a way to rationalize how friendship and affective ties might play a central role in her professional work, but, as the discussion progressed, it became apparent that her lingering concerns may be more directly rooted in her own disciplinary training: "I'm also trained as a historian and maybe that's part of it too—a desire to remain objective?"[31] By the end of our exchange on this topic (in which she had initially rejected the idea that friendship might not only matter but be integral), Darms stated, "I truly believe that my relationship to the donors, my friendships, the fact that I was in Olympia when all this stuff was going on, puts me in a better position to build this collection."[32]

If Darms was initially hesitant to acknowledge the importance of her personal connection to the donors, her donors were entirely forthcoming about the essential role their connection to Darms has played in the collection's development. Johanna Fateman explained, "It definitely helped that Lisa is a close friend, and that I trusted her to have a sensitivity to the issues surrounding the project."[33] Similarly, for Hanna, the decision to donate her papers to Fales Library appeared to be directly linked to Darms's position there as senior archivist. "I really don't think I would've been interested if someone else, besides Lisa Darms, had approached me," explained Hanna. "It just felt like the universe lined up and it was meant to be."[34] In a sense, the universe *had* lined up, as the following origin story recounted by Hanna suggests:

> Lisa and I and our friend Johanna had gone to an event about feminism and the archive at Fales before she got a job there and I LOVED Marvin, the head of Fales, from the second he started talking. As we were leaving Jo and I started joking about how great it would be if they did a Riot Grrrl Archive so we could get rid of all the stuff we'd kept over the years. 6 months later Lisa was hired as Fales' senior archivist and called us up saying "What if a Riot Grrrl Archive really existed, would you all be involved?" I was completely thrilled. It was a dream come true scenario.[35]

While Darms emphasizes her historical connection to Riot Grrrl (for example, the fact that she was in Olympia in the early 1990s when Riot Grrrl was taking shape), Hanna emphasizes that Darms's present connection to the donors is at least as essential as her historical link to the movement: "I really trust Lisa's intelligence and her ability to make great things happen. . . . Her proximity to the places and events that shaped RG make things a lot easier for sure, but to me, that's secondary. More important is the fact that she has a great sense of humor which I think is pretty important if you're going to put something together of this magnitude."[36]

Although many women who came of age in the 1990s and beyond feel a personal connection to the papers in the Riot Grrrl Collection, it is not necessarily *their* archive. That so many women have interpreted the collection as an archive of an entire generation of feminists rather than a collection that contains several individuals' personal papers, however, is not entirely surprisingly. Documents and artifacts connected to traditionally marginalized groups have historically been more likely to enter archives because they represent a demographic or cultural phenomenon than on basis of their connection to individuals. Many collections of women's archival materials, for example, are comprised of diaries and letters written by anonymous or unknown women writers rather than writers who gained notoriety for their work; the materials are valuable because they tell us something about the conditions of women's everyday lives in a particular era and not because they tell us something about the individual writers. In many respects, the zine collections at both Barnard College and Duke University extend this tradition of collection development in women's archives. While both collections contain zines produced by or about the women whose papers are also housed in the Riot Grrrl Collection, it is important to bear in mind that even the same zine may represent something different in the collections at Barnard College or Duke University than it does in the collection at Fales Library. As Jenna Freedman, the founder and librarian responsible for the Barnard Zine Library, emphasizes, her collection is one that belongs to and represents "every girl." A zine by or about Kathleen Hanna in the Barnard Zine Library is there as part of a larger and still growing collection of zines by girls and women and gender-queer subjects. By contrast, Darms emphasizes that her collection focuses on Riot Grrrl and more specifically on the papers of some women connected to the movement's development. In this context, a zine by or about Hanna is not representative of DIY publishing or "girl power," as it might be elsewhere. At Fales Library, it is one document among many that tells us something about Hanna's development as an artist, performer, and activist.

By creating a collection with a mandate "to collect unique materials that provide documentation of the creative process of *individuals* and the chronology of the movement overall" (emphasis my own), Darms is not only creating the first collection of Riot Grrrl *papers*, but she is also effectively relocating and redefining Riot Grrrl in ways that will profoundly impact how writers will consider Riot Grrrl and particular Riot Grrrl figures in the future.[37] This collection's development, including the combined geographic and symbolic acts of relocation it entails, represents a realignment of Riot Grrrl that highlights both the movement's intellectual and artistic lineages and, by extension, the archive's status as a historiographic technology.

Continental Drift

Like many observers, when I first heard about the development of the Riot Grrrl Collection at Fales Library, I immediately questioned the choice of location. After all, while Riot Grrrls were active in New York in the early 1990s, the city was neither an early site of Riot Grrrl activity nor was Riot Grrrl NYC necessarily typical of the form Riot Grrrl scenes took in other cities.[38] More importantly, I questioned whether Riot Grrrl could have emerged when it did and with such impact had it been conceived by a group of college-age women at a small liberal arts college in New York rather than one located in a bucolic setting on the Northwest Coast. Beyond the fact that finding space on a stage in New York is presumably more difficult than finding space on a stage in Olympia, especially if you are a young women with a limited performance history, other circumstances would have made New York an unlikely scene for Riot Grrrl's emergence in the early 1990s.

From 1989 to 1992, while Riot Grrrl was taking shape at Evergreen State College in Olympia, rising rates of HIV infection and HIV-related deaths combined with government apathy at the municipal, state, and federal levels had left New York's downtown scene caught in a cycle of death, mourning, and activism. Young queer women were by no means immune to the impact of AIDS and the political and cultural movements it incited, even if few were ever infected by the virus. As revealed in the interviews that comprise Jim Hubbard and Sarah Schulman's ACT UP Oral History Project, an extensive online archive of interviews and interview transcripts with a surviving generation of AIDS activist, lesbians, perhaps especially in New York, were deeply involved in ACT UP and the many allied organizations and collective projects it generated in the late 1980s to early 1990s.[39] On this basis, it seems reasonable to conclude that to be a young queer feminist in Olympia and New York in the late 1980s to early 1990s meant radically different things. What was pressing in New York's downtown scene during this period was day-to-day survival, making it difficult, if not impossible, to imagine the conditions under which a girl-centered movement could have emerged in this context.

This is not to suggest, however, that Riot Grrrl was entirely untouched by either the impact of AIDS or the activism the crisis engendered. This indirect influence is apparent in the following passage from an unpublished essay by Hanna (now housed in Johanna Fateman's files in the Riot Grrrl Collection at Fales Library). Reflecting on her formation, Hanna writes:

> I came of age as an activist/artist during the short lived
> media hey day of ACT UP, Queer Nation, The Guerilla girls
> and WAC. I watched these groups using confrontational,
> theatrical tactics to disrupt "the powers that be" and liked
> a lot of what I saw. At times I tried to use the same kinds
> of strategies within the punk/feminist community I was
> very much a part of at the time. Sometimes doing this drew
> much needed action and discussion to the issues I cared
> about most.[40]

For Hanna, ACT UP, emblematic of a particular moment of media savvy queer and feminist activism in the late 1980s to early 1990s, exemplified how the creative deployment of the media might be used to achieve both aesthetic and political objectives. In *Girls to the Front*, Marcus also emphasizes the indirect influence organizations like ACT UP had on Riot Grrrl. As she explains, it is no coincidence that Angela Seguel—best known for posing naked with "every girl is a Riot Grrrl" written on her torso in the British magazine *i-D*—had spent time engaging in ACT UP activism. As Marcus emphasizes, "Angela knew, from her time in ACT UP, that a carefully orchestrated image could say a lot,"[41] and the infamous photograph she staged for *i-D* exhibited just such awareness.

Thus, while there is no doubt that some Riot Grrrls were involved in or at least impacted by the political struggles reshaping queer and feminist communities in the late 1980s to early 1990s, it seems likely that Olympia's location *away* from the dire battles facing gay men and lesbians in New York, San Francisco, and other large urban centers at the time was at least a factor in Riot Grrrl's development. Given the geographic specificity of Riot Grrrl's emergence, however, on what basis might we justify the movement of the Riot Grrrl papers to the Fales Library and Special Collections in New York two decades later? If Riot Grrrl could not have emerged in New York when it did (at least not in the same form), what makes Fales Library such an appropriate home now? This question is particularly significant given that the Downtown Collection, with which the Riot Grrrl Collection holds most in common, was founded at the height of the AIDS crisis in 1993, in part owing to Fales Library and Special Collection's Director Marvin Taylor, who realized the urgent need to create a home where the papers and artifacts of recently deceased artists could be housed and properly preserved.[42]

If Taylor's impetus to create the Downtown Collection was the result of an urgent and even dire need, Darms has had the privilege of developing the Riot Grrrl Collection under much less pressing circumstances. When she considers the question of location, Darms first points to the practical challenges one faces when attempting to establish any special collection. "Perhaps, in an ideal world, they would be in an institution in Olympia or Washington, DC," she admits, "but you need an institution that is committed to preserving these materials in the long term and that requires institutional backing and subject knowledge to support the materials."[43] Darms also emphasizes that New York is more accessible to researchers than other possible locations, such as Olympia, DC, or Minneapolis, and may even benefit

from a certain "neutrality" because it is *not* one of these locations, which are more synonymous with Riot Grrrl's early development.[44] Beyond such practical considerations, there are other
issues at stake. Locating the collection in Olympia, Minneapolis,
or DC may honor the movement's geographic specificity at its
moment of origin, but privileging geography also risks reinforc-
ing the idea of Riot Grrrl as a subculture. After all, subcultures
have historically been defined along the basis of not only style
and cultural practices but also geography. This is evident in both
British and North American theorizing on subcultures, which
have frequently privileged and even romanticized the specific
neighborhoods that have allegedly given birth to subcultures,
from London's East End to New York's Harlem and the Bronx.[45]
Rather than privilege geography, the Riot Grrrl Collection privileges the movement's historical lineages. Once again, in this
respect, the collection's adjacency to Fales Library's existing special collections, especially the Downtown Collection, is significant, but Darms explains the difference: because "the Downtown
Collection is obviously so specific to New York," the connection
is "more of an intellectual and aesthetic relationship."[46]

It is important to acknowledge that the question of relocation is by no means a question unique to the Riot Grrrl Collection at Fales Library. Echoing other theorists on the archive, in
the final chapter of *An Archive of Feelings*, Cvetkovich concludes,
"The history of any archive is a history of space."[47] But as she further emphasizes, gay and lesbian archives have been especially
engaged in transforming spaces because "their existence has been
dependent on the possibility of making private spaces—such as
rooms in people's homes—public."[48] On this basis, she further
argues that gay and lesbian archives are an "intriguing locus of
debates about institutionalization and the tensions around assimilation in gay and lesbian politics."[49] In other words, the archive
is not simply a space that promises to preserve traces of marginal
subjects' lives but also a locus that holds the power to integrate
and even "mainstream" such subjects. Much of the controversy
surrounding the Riot Grrrl Collection has focused on whether the

collection represents a form of institutional assimilation. While the critique is not entirely surprising, it rests on the assumption that Riot Grrrl, once upon a time, existed *outside* the academy, an assumption by no means consistent with either the movement's history or its mandate.

Institutionalization and Assimilation

As previously emphasized, upon news of the Riot Grrrl Collection's development, many bloggers celebrated not only the development of an archival collection dedicated to Riot Grrrl but also the appearance of a new destination for fans. A response to a posting on *The Girls Are . . .* blog read: "How awesome! Yes, roadtrip!" *The Girls Are . . .* agreed: "Seriously, I think I [could] craft a roadtrip around this one activity!"[50] If the initial public response to the Riot Grrrl Collection was marked by preliminary plans for pilgrimages to Fales Library, then as the conditions of the collection became more apparent some fans responded with disappointment. In November 2010, the following tongue-and-cheek article appeared in the *Village Voice*, which may have further contributed to the rumors and confusion about the collection's access policy:

> . . . the collection is only open to "qualified researchers' (a/k/a academes) to view in the Fales" reading room. For the rest of us unqualified schlubs, Darms is also looking to sponsor symposiums and conferences centered around grrrl cultural/feminism/queer studies as well as possible exhibitions and screenings.[51]

While the *Village Voice* piece was presumably not intended as a critique, responses on their website and subsequent online debates suggest that at least some fans considered the collection's access policy at odds with Riot Grrrl's central tenets. On the *Village Voice* website, for example, Fran responded, presumably under the impression that Hanna had never agreed to the terms of the collection, with the following post: "i don't think that kathleen hanna would of donated this collection if she had [known] that it was only accessible to the educated elite!"[52] Darms not surprisingly rejects suggestions that the decision to locate the Riot Grrrl papers in a special collections library at a private university is necessarily problematic:

> [Fales Library has] a relatively open policy for access, but it still needs to be an appointment made through me or another curator, and you still need to have a scholarly project. Scholarly is something we interpret broadly, because many of our researchers are artists. . . . I have made sure that the donations have happened with an understanding that the materials will be accessed for scholarly projects. This has been the motivation for the donors so far—a recognition that the materials will support research. They haven't donated their materials to make them more accessible to fans.[53]

This is not to suggest that the backlash has been entirely easy for Darms. She admits, "it is difficult for me because my background is an anti-institutional, DIY, fuck the institution philosophy."[54] Darms adds that, although she has not had any resistance from donors yet, "maybe the potential donors who aren't responding have some qualms about placing their materials in an institution."[55] The women who have agreed to donate their papers clearly share much with Darms in their thinking about the archive.

Hanna's and Fateman's support for the collection's development, for example, also emphasizes the importance of preservation. "I didn't want to give all my stuff to some collective that might close down in a month and throw my stuff in the trash," explained Hanna.[56] When asked about the collection's institutional location, Fateman also emphasized the desire to place her papers in an established archive: "There are DIY archives but are they committed to preservation? Likely not in the way an institutional collection is committed to preservation."[57] In addition to emphasizing the importance of preservation and the fact that institutional archives, such as Fales Library, are typically better equipped to carry out preservation than collections located in community settings, which frequently lack proper storage facilities, Darms, Fateman, and Hanna offer shared responses, consistent with at least two important tenets of Riot Grrrl, to critiques of the collection's location.

First, the collection, which will provide access to a wide range of academic and independent researchers but at the discretion of library staff, appears to reflect the Riot Grrrl movement's own commitment to open access *within limits*. On this account, it is by no means insignificant that in defense of the collection's institutional context, Hanna draws a parallel between the collection and contemporary zine production:

> It's like people who make paper fanzines in 2010 are making a specific choice to reach a smaller audience than maybe a blog could, it's an artistic decision. One that has to do with having a tactile object that exists in the real world and can be physically passed from person to person. Choosing an archive that has an intended audience and isn't for everyone is a similar choice to me. Also, since most of the stuff I donated was created before the internet, I would prefer it be viewed physically and in context. If it was open to everyone little bits of it would inevitably end up on the internet, and I don't really want rough drafts of shit I wrote twenty years ago popping up online ahistorical style.[58]

Second, Darms emphasizes the importance of understanding that this collection, unlike existing collections of Riot Grrrl related materials, contains the papers of individuals and not simply zines, recordings, and artwork that have already been in circulation, if only in the semipublic textual communities of zine producers.[59] As a result, it requires more care and sensitivity and hence a heightened degree of what some fans perceive as institutional gatekeeping:

> Much of the material is very personal and with the figures involved, it could be very divisive if certain information was freely circulated—we're collecting journals, letters,

even legal documents. So I don't think that it's material that really needs to be accessible to anyone. I feel strongly about that in terms of archival reading rooms, even if it's not a popular way to view library practice but in terms of the archive, this is really standard practice.[60]

This is not to suggest that Darms is uncommitted to supporting venues where Riot Grrrl materials are more readily accessible. In fact, she sees herself working in collaboration with other archivists and librarians building Riot Grrrl related collections: "there are still going to be venues where people can go to look at zines and that's really important to me. That's what Jenna Freedman is doing up at Barnard. But people are also taking it upon themselves to scan zines and create online archives. Those online archives may not last very long but it does create a way to make the zines accessible now."[61]

In addition to extending Riot Grrrl's practice of facilitating access to information without entirely relinquishing control over its circulation, the Riot Grrrl Collection extends the movement's longstanding practice of tactically deploying the academic apparatus. As Hanna explains, "Universities have more money than most left political groups and personally I don't want lefty feminist groups spending their resources maintaining archives when they could be doing more important things."[62] In many respects, Riot Grrrl has always operated as a parasitic presence on the academy, never colonizing its host but consistently deploying its resources (intellectual and material) to further its own agenda. Once again, in this respect, it is important to recognize that the movement emerged in and around a college campus. Known for its innovative curriculum and commitment to collaborative and self-designed programs of study,[63] Evergreen State College not only served as an institutional base from which to initiate specific projects (for example, a Riot Grrrl zine distribution network was started as an independent study course at the college),[64] but, at least indirectly, it also supplied the movement with resources from copy paper and other zine-making supplies to space.

In the early 1990s, however, Riot Grrrl was doing much more than leaching the academy of material resources. Referring to the early years of Riot Grrrl and her own college experience at Evergreen, Darms emphasizes that "a lot of the materials people were reading were academic. It was a really smart movement, a well informed movement."[65] While academic feminist discourses by no means had been absent from an earlier generation's community newspapers and journals, the range of scholarly discourses in nonrefereed second wave publications and forms of cultural production was limited. Outside the academy, and at times even inside the academy, it was *de rigueur* for second wave feminists to eschew theoretical discourses perceived as "elitist," "difficult," and "inaccessible." By the early 1990s, however, the divide between so-called "academic" and "grassroots" feminisms was already dissolving, and Riot Grrrl was what it was because it emerged at this particular theoretical and political moment,[66] when fixed notions of identity were rapidly giving way to a more nuanced and complex understandings of the subject—the moment when everyone appeared to be celebrating both the "smartness" and political potential of irony, parody, pastiche, and appropriation. After nearly two decades of steady political gains by feminists both inside and outside the academy, the early 1990s was also a privileged moment, a brief interval in which young feminists could afford to embrace emerging theoretical positions while remaining fully committed to most of the tenets of second wave feminist politics. And perhaps this is why Riot Grrrl, from the onset, sought to embrace and even celebrate rather than eschew contradictions.

On my first trip to access the Riot Grrrl Collection at Fales Library in February 2011, I spoke to Darms, whom I had originally interviewed for this chapter in June 2010 (before the collection had been made available to researchers). After hearing about the form this chapter was taking, she directed me to five file folders of photocopied articles in the still unprocessed papers of Kathleen Hanna. Although it is not entirely clear at what point Hanna started to collect the materials contained in the files, the range of materials not only points to the breadth of the artist's reading and influences but also offers insight into the intellectual and political orientation of the Riot Grrrl movement. I offer an abbreviated list of some of the articles and clippings found in Hanna's files. The list, to be clear, is not a finding aid but simply a selection of what I chose to record while looking through the first three of the five folders. In some cases, I have added notes, including notes about the bibliographical information, marginalia and mark-ups that appear on the photocopied materials.

David James, "Hardcore: Cultural Resistance in the Postmodern"

Kathy Acker, "Realism for the Cause of Future Revolution"

Chris Straayer, "The She-man: Postmodern bi-sexed performance in film and video" (copied from *Screen*, Autumn 1990)

Helene Cixous, "The Laugh of the Medusa" (copied from *Signs 1*, no.4, 1976)

A book review of Derrida's *Glas* (marked with pink highlighting)

Gregg Bordowitz, "Dense Moments"

Hazel V. Carby, "The Politics of Difference"

Hilton Als, "The Furies"

Robin West, "Pornography as a Legal Text" (note on back includes references to *Lesbian Ethics* by Sarah Lucia Hoagland, *Daring to be Bad* by Alic Echols, *Not for Sale* by Laura Cottingham, *Illusions of Postmodernism* by Terry Eagleton, *Yes* by Yoko Ono, and the *Collected works Felix Gonzales Torres*)

Review of *Kathy Goes to Haiti, My Death My Life by Pier Paulo Pasolini,* and *Florida* by Kathy Acker

William Burroughs, "Is the Body Obsolete" (published in the *Whole Earth Review* in 1989)

Kathy Acker, "Dead Doll Humility" (copied from *Postmodern Culture*, 1990)

An article about the Montreal massacre published in
McLean's (Dec. 18, 1989)

Fragment from "Bodies that Matter" by Judith Butler
("Phantasmatic Identification")

Heinrich Himmler, "A Body of Authority by Susan Griffin"
(*Whole Earth Review*, 1989)

A pamphlet on abortion rights

Ann Cvetkovich "Sexual Trauma/Queer Memory: Incest,
Lesbianism, and Therapeutic Culture" (copied from *GLQ*)

Laura Kipnis, "(Male) Desire and (Female) Disgust Reading
Hustler" (extensive notes on back)

Excerpts from *Z Magazine* (1999)

Nikki Craft, "In Defense of Disobedience" (copied from
Fight Back)

bell hooks, "Beauty Laid Bare: Aesthetics in the Ordinary"[67]

If we accept the fact that, given Hanna's place as one founder of
Riot Grrrl, her personal reading inventory is by no means inconsequential to understanding the political and intellectual roots
of the movement, then I maintain the above inventory is worth
considering at length. First, several articles point to the influence of deconstructionist, poststructuralist, and postmodern
theorizing (for example, the reviews of books by and about the
Derrida, the excerpt from Butler's *Bodies that Matter*, the copied
articles by and about French feminist theorists, and the chapter
of Terry Eagleton's *Illusions of Postmodernism*). Second, there is
substantial evidence that Hanna, like many of her peers at the
time, was still grappling with second wave feminist debates (for
example, Laura Kipnis's article on reading *Hustler* and Hazel V.
Carby's discussion on the "politics of difference"). At the same
time, the inventory points to the strong influence of queer theory
and politics (see Gregg Bordowitz). These scholarly articles notably intermingle with news clippings (the article about the massacre of fourteen women in a classroom at École Polytechnique

SUBJECT TOPICS

- Alternative Spaces (Arts facilities).
- Art | v Exhibitions.
- Art | x Exhibitions | z New York (State) | z New York.
- Art | x Experimental methods.
- Artists and community | z United States.
- Dance music | z United States.
- Electronic music.
- Evergreen State College.
- Feminism and art.
- Feminism.
- Feminist music.
- Gender Identity | z United States.
- Interactive art.
- Lesbians | z United States.
- Multimedia (art).
- Musicians | y 1990–2000.
- Politics in art.
- Punk culture.
- Punk rock music.
- Riot grrrl movement.
- Women artists | z United States.
- Women's rights
- Zines

FIGURE 3.1 Subject topics listed in the finding aid to the Kathleen Hanna Papers, Riot Grrrl Collection, Fales Library and Special Collections.

in Montréal on December 6, 1989) and features from the radical press (the articles copied from the *Whole Earth Review* and *Z Magazine*). Finally, there are references to a particular lineage of avant-garde writers and artists through the references to William Burroughs, Yoko Ono, Hilton Als, and Kathy Acker.

While Hanna's papers at the Riot Grrrl Collection paint a deeply complex picture of Riot Grrrl's relationship to hardcore, punk, feminism, popular culture, critical theory, and avant-garde literature and art, to date, few scholars of Riot Grrrl have accounted for this complexity. I admit that my own research on Riot Grrrl, beginning with a thesis on girl zines in 1994, is by no means exempt from this criticism. Looking back on my thesis (for the first time in well over a decade), I discovered that, although I recognized that the girl zine networks at the center of my research were inspired by, but not exclusively connected to, Riot Grrrl and further acknowledged the danger of constructing girl zine networks as a manifestation of a single youth culture or subculture, when discussing Riot Grrrl I generally referred to the movement as a subculture. My early research on Riot Grrrl, however, was consistent with other early studies on the movement, including Joanne Gottlieb and Gayle Wald's article, "Smells like Teen Spirit: Riot Grrrl, Revolution and Women in Independent Rock," which appeared in Tricia Rose and Andrew Ross's edited collection, *Microphone Fiends* in 1994. In what was likely the first scholarly publication on Riot Grrrl, Gottlieb and Wald maintain that "from its inception, Riot Grrrl emerges as a bona fide subculture."[68] They draw generously on the work of Angela McRobbie and other British subcultural studies theorists, such as Simon Frith and Dick Hebdige, to support their depiction of Riot Grrrl as a "bona fide subculture." Wald extends this position in her 1998 *Signs* article, "Just a Girl?: Rock Music, Feminism, and the Cultural Construction of Female Youth," referring to Riot Grrrl as a "female youth subculture,"[69] and a "musical subculture."[70] In many respects, it was by no means misleading to construct Riot Grrrl as a subculture. With its own distinctive style, music, discourse, and social codes, the movement fit neatly into existing case studies on subcultures, including Hebdige's studies on British punk and McRobbie's studies of the British rave scene. However, as Fateman emphasizes, "Many academics viewed RG rather romantically and wishfully. . . . There was a desire to see it as a spontaneous radical feminist teen movement that had a kind of 'street cred,' rather than something that was connected to campus women's centers, take back the night marches, feminist scholarship, and avant-garde literature."[71]

The problem of bringing a subcultural studies model to bear on Riot Grrrl, then, may have less to do with what such a model imposed on the movement and more to do with what the model effectively obscured about the movement's origins, influences, and long-term impacts. As Fateman observes, "The 'girl gang' image was cultivated by some within the movement, and it was 'real' in terms of certain guerilla tactics and punk antics, but Riot Grrrl was also an aesthetic thing (rhetorical, theorized)."[72] Fateman adds, "Its status as a political movement and social phenomenon still seems to overshadow its status as an artistic movement. Its products still aren't discussed much *as art*."[73] In *Gender in the Music Industry* (2007), Marion Leonard also addresses this oversight. She recognizes that "riot grrrl's development parallels the way a number of youth subcultures have established themselves. It emerges from within 'underground' music circles; was promoted through gigs, events and zine networks; and was greeted with considerable levels of fascination by the mass media."[74] Leonard goes on, however, to warn that applying this model of analysis to Riot Grrrl is misleading. Emphasizing that "one of the flaws of subcultural theory has been its tenacious grasp of the concept of delinquency," she observes, "Youth subcultures have often been positioned as oppositional to the 'parent culture' and thereby at odds with societal norms."[75] This approach, she emphasizes, has "particular relevance to Riot Grrrl" because "to place riot grrrl in a tradition of delinquent youth theory would be to ignore the nature of its protest and dismiss its feminist objectives as mere teen dissent."[76] Again, the scope and range of radical literatures, critical theory, and avant-garde works included and referenced in Hanna's files in the Riot Grrrl Collection suggests that at least at its point of origin, Riot Grrrl was already far too self-reflexive and entangled in the institutions and industries it sought to occupy and critique to be understood simply through a framework of youth dissent.

Thus, on the one hand, the fact that the Riot Grrrl Collection is unavailable to every fan on a pilgrimage may appear to come into conflict with Riot Grrrl's commitment to locating girls and young women as agents of knowledge and cultural production and social change. On the other hand, the collection's development is entirely in keeping with the movement's longstanding relationship to the academy. Like the movement itself, the collection reflects a tactical deployment of the academy's resources and represents an attempt to use the academy as a means to shape how the movement will be taken up in a larger public sphere. In our interview, Darms reflected briefly on her own early experience of Riot Grrrl. Her recollection reveals the extent to which the movement is not only indebted to punk but to multiple and overlapping aesthetic and intellectual traditions. Indeed, she emphasizes these complex lineages while simultaneously making a strong case for why the Riot Grrrl papers are at home among existing collections at Fales Library:

> For me, Riot Grrrl is absolutely an off-shoot of punk. I don't think that everyone experienced it that way, but historically, it was definitely a reaction to punk and the failures of gender in that radical aesthetic. But there are also important intellectual connections. Take, for example, the Semiotexte Collection. The people who are in that collection, like Kathy Acker and Eileen Myles, are people who women involved with Riot Grrrl were reading and inspired by. But there's also other connections—even the little pocket Baudrillard that I remember seeing at a friend's house for the first time when I was still in Olympia—it was like an introduction to a whole world. The same day I saw the Baudrillard, my friend played me Kathleen's spoken word 7--inch. So in my mind, there are many connections both aesthetically and intellectually. Also, both collections [The Downtown Collection and the Semiotexte Collection] are very queer.[77]

From punk to Semiotexte, from Myles to Baudrillard, from a college-age Kathleen Hanna to New York's downtown art scene,

Darms covers immense ground here, but in so doing she effectively demonstrates the slippages and connections that are integral to understanding Riot Grrrl. Far from a "bona fide subculture," as Gottlieb and Wald argue in their early theorizing on the movement, Darms represents Riot Grrrl as queer feminist hybrid of punk, continental philosophy, feminism, and avant-garde literary and art traditions. Thus, the Riot Grrrl Collection at Fales Library represents neither a form of institutionalization nor assimilation but rather foregrounds something that was always already part of the Riot Grrrl movement—its link to both the academic apparatus and to some of the theoretical and aesthetic movements it has sustained.

Avant-garde Heritage

The idea that a radical movement might have an "avant-garde heritage" is, I admit, at least somewhat contradictory. If we understand the avant-garde along Bourdieu's lines, then avant-garde movements are by definition *without* a "heritage" or "lineage" to which they can truly lay claim because "'young' writers, i.e., those less advanced in the process of consecration . . . will refuse everything their 'elders' . . . are and do, and in particular all their indices of *social ageing*, starting with the signs of consecration, internal (academies, etc.) or external (success)."[78] But this, evidently, is a perspective that is either no longer relevant to theorizing on how avant-gardes are formed or one in which Riot Grrrl stands as a notable exception.

As Fateman emphasizes, "Some Riot Grrrls (especially after the *Newsweek*, *USA Today*, *Sassy* articles) were quite young and knew nothing about Kathy Acker, Karen Finley, Diamanda Galas, Barbara Kruger, etc but those in the most notorious Riot Grrrl bands most certainly did."[79] It seems unlikely that a song like "Hot Topic," released on Le Tigre's debut album in 1998, could exist without such an awareness:

Carol Rama and Eleanor Antin
Yoko Ono and Carolee Schneeman

You're getting old, that's what they'll say, but
Don't give a damn I'm listening anyway[80]

The song mentions a myriad of other artists, writers, performers, and scholars, including modernist icon Gertrude Stein, contemporary poet and experimental prose writer Eileen Myles, and celebrated late twentieth-century artist David Wojnarowicz. Notably absent from the list of venerated influences is Kathy Acker; however, Hanna's connection to Acker is particularly illustrative.

Among the articles and newspaper clippings Hanna chose to keep and include in her donation to the Riot Grrrl Collection are dozens of articles by and about Acker, but the Hanna-Acker connection is also an exception. In contrast to other connections between established innovative writers and artists and the Riot Grrrl movement, this connection has already been recognized as part of Riot Grrrl history. In a 2002 article in the *Village Voice*, in which Acker is described as "a riot grrrl ahead of her time,"[81] Hanna discusses a fated weekend workshop with Acker in Seattle in 1990. As the legend goes, Acker told Hanna, "If you want to be heard, why are you doing spoken word? You should be in a band."[82] As we all know, Hanna went home and started a band, and Acker was right—bands get more airplay than poetry. Whether Acker would have embraced the idea that she was a "riot grrrl ahead of her time" is unclear. After all, Acker was very much an individual, not a movement. Nevertheless, as a tough, sexually complicated, outspoken, punk writer and performer who had found a way to play with the boys and espouse feminist politics without being coopted by either camp, Acker was an ideal role model for Hanna and her peers. She exemplified what it meant to be both punk and feminist, political and theoretically engaged, a public figure but by no means an object of media manipulation.

While the Acker influence on Hanna was the result of a direct encounter, for other Riot Grrrls, the influence of Acker and other avant-garde women writers and performers, such as Eileen Myles and Karen Findley, may have been neither as direct nor as widely acknowledged, but it is apparent in the work nevertheless. In *Girls to the Front*, Marcus makes a point of foregrounding these connections, and to her credit she carefully avoids implying that they were merely about young women searching for feisty feminist role models in the late years of the second wave feminist movement. As Marcus emphasizes, connections, such as the one between Hanna and Acker, were first and foremost intellectual and aesthetic:

> Acker's insolent, demanding fictions tackled female sexuality head-on and took an ax to literary form. In *Blood and Guts in High School*, the 1978 novel that got Kathleen hooked, a young girl begs her father for sex, joins a gang, has two abortions, and goes to a Contortions concert—all in the first forty-three pages. The story is told in a fragmented, deadpan way, through shifting points of view and collage: fairy tales, scripts, poems, line drawings of men's and women's genitals, pages from a Persian-language workbook. *Blood and Guts* suggested that the realities of women's lives, especially with regard to sexuality and abuse, were too complicated to be told through typical narrative. Only contradictions, ruptures and refusals stood a chance of conveying the truth.[83]

Directly or indirectly, with few exceptions, early Riot Grrrl writing, such as the writing found in many of the zines published between 1990 and 1994, reflects this recognition that women's lives, especially women's experiences of sexuality and abuse, are too complicated to be expressed in linear narrative prose. As an example, consider the following passage that appears in the middle of an abuse narrative published in a Riot Grrrl zine from this era:[84] "Is my real life pain and abuse good enough to be an article in a fucking fanzine for you to read WHO ARE YOU? stop reading this. I said STOP RITE NOW. you're still reading. its okay you know I really want you to."[85] The use of such interruptions in a narrative that otherwise may be read as a typical confessional piece of writing on sexual abuse was by no means uncommon in Riot Grrrl writing at the time. In fact, a distinctive marker of early Riot Grrrl writing was its disjunctive narrative style, which frequently included insertions intended to make the reader aware of their complicity in the production of the text and at times their potential voyeurism. By extension, early Riot Grrrl writing had a tendency to destabilize the speaking subject, often rendering the writer's intentions ambiguous and even inaccessible. As demonstrated above, the writing was also marked by notable typographical innovations and grammatical irregularities, making it difficult for readers to ignore the extent to which language is a scene of power, regulation, and constraint that must be interrogated. Thus, while one could read such writing as a form of life writing or autobiography, the repeated use of these conventions suggests that early Riot Grrrl writers were by no means working on the assumption that language is a mere vehicle for representation. In this respect, their writing arguably shared much more in common with the disturbing, clever, and disjunctive narrative presented in Acker's *Blood and Guts in High School* than with texts typically theorized as life writing or autobiography. My point here, however, is not that the unidentified writer of the above passage was necessarily directly influenced by Acker (as we know Hanna was) but rather that there is a substantial basis upon which to read such texts as more rhetorically and aesthetically sophisticated than they have typically been read. After all, many early Riot Grrrl writers (note, I am choosing to refer to them as *writers* rather than *zinesters* here) were, like Acker and her contemporaries in the avant-garde writing scenes in New York and San Francisco, committed to creating a textual space where competing tendencies, narratives, truths, styles, and aesthetics could coexist; this, however, is something that has been largely ignored by researchers of Riot Grrrl. The question remains: *why* have critics generally assumed that Riot Grrrls were doing what they were doing (on the page and the stage) more or less naively, without a sense of the innovative literary and art movements that preceded them?

One could easily conclude that the relative neglect of Riot Grrrl cultural production as literature and art reflects the general status of women writers and artists, especially those affiliated with so-called avant-garde movements. After all, even when women have been present from the onset, such movements often have been primarily or exclusively attributed to one or more male "geniuses" (hence, the hero worship of the Tzaras, Duchamps, and Debords). Following these lines, one might assume that the problem is nothing less than the "girl" in Riot Grrrl, but the relative absence of controversy surrounding the development of the Riot Grrrl Collection at Fales Library suggests that, in many respects, Riot Grrrl has already been recognized as a historically significant cultural phenomenon. The problem is not necessarily one of recognition but of the mode of that recognition, and as such gender alone cannot account for the oversight in question.

Returning to the question of Riot Grrrl writing, it is important to recognize that, with few exceptions, researchers have tended to ignore the specificity of Riot Grrrl writing by classifying this writing within the broader category of girl zine writing. Viewed through this lens, most apparent are the common issues Riot Grrrl and other girl zines address (for example, abuse, eating disorders, sexuality, and so on) rather than the mode of address or the procedures at work in the texts. In other words, content is invariably privileged over form, pushing aesthetic questions to the margins. This is evident in Alison Piepmeier's *Girl Zines: Making Media, Doing Feminism*. Notably absent from Piepmeier's study is any extended discussion of zine writing in relation to pastiche, détournement, appropriation, or questions of authorship. Rather than take up this writing as literature, Piepmeier understands both Riot Grrrl writing and other girl zine writing primarily in relation to its social and political content. When aesthetics are taken up more explicitly, it is in relation to concepts such as "bricolage," an anthropological term and one with considerable currency in subcultural studies.[86] Although this is by no means a reason to overlook Piepmeier's important study on girl zines, it reminds us—as Darms evidently hopes to foreground through the development of the Riot Grrrl Collection—that context matters and that context more specifically holds the potential to produce the critical perspectives that amass around a given cultural product to determine its status as a symbolic object in the field of cultural production.

Recasting the Field of Cultural Production through the Archive

To be clear, the objective of this chapter was not to rewrite Riot Grrrl as an avant-garde movement. After all, such a history merits an entire book, and it is a book that should be written. I wish to highlight here that the Riot Grrrl Collection at Fales Library and Special Collections holds the potential to facilitate precisely such a rewriting of Riot Grrrl. On this basis, we can conclude that the collection's development demonstrates how archives are implicated in, what Bourdieu describes as, "position-takings." In other words, the collection reveals how archives are part and parcel of the process of endowing works of art and literature as well as *individual* artists and writers with varying degrees of cultural capital and prestige. If the archive is integral to such "position-takings," however, it is to the extent that it is or holds the possibility to be engaged in the production of critics and their writings. As demonstrated throughout this chapter, the Riot Grrrl Collection not only draws attention to the role of the archive in the field of cultural production but also challenges Bourdieu's understanding of how avant-gardes are established within the field by revealing how an avant-garde may be established through a strategic alliance with the past rather than through a "pushing back" of one's predecessors. Finally, in addition to offering an occasion to challenge Bourdieu's theorizing (for example, his oversight of the archive's position in the field of cultural production and assumptions about the conditions under which avant-gardes are formed), the development of the Riot Grrrl Collection offers an occasion to challenge both feminist critiques of Bourdieu and perspectives on the feminist subfield.

As a response to Bourdieu's theorizing on the field of cultural production, in her 2002 article, "Feminist Periodicals and the Production of Cultural Value," Barbara Godard contends, "Gender . . . is not a category that Bourdieu introduces into his model of complex social stratification. For him, distinctions operate primarily within differentials of class."[87] Women, Godard observes, are only taken into account by Bourdieu as a target market of cultural products rather than as producers. Bourdieu's oversight is especially relevant to understanding the status of "high art," under which the so-called avant-garde, innovative, and experimental are typically grouped:

> Because of its relative difficulty or rarity, the "high-art" produced by the field of "restricted production" is considered "pure" and functions as an element of social prestige. Such anti-economic behaviour paradoxically constitutes "symbolic capital": disinterest in "'economic' profits" works dialectically to consolidate "a capital of consecration" by "making a name for oneself." . . . Through the prestige of a signature or trademark, those agents can "consecrate objects" and so create cultural value across fields. [88]

To illustrate, we might consider the success of some cultural movements/industries that emerged simultaneous to Riot Grrrl in the early to mid 1990s, which include "indie" film and music and open source programming. By initially rejecting profit as a primary motivation for their acts of creation, these largely male-dominated movements/industries gained a caché that was in turn soon converted into cultural prestige and economic capital (hence, the sudden trend of established Hollywood directors choosing to direct and produce "indie" films for prestige and profit or the for-profit redeployment of forms of digital creativity that were anti-economic at their point of origin). By comparison, Riot Grrrl, which opted out of established publishing and recording venues to embrace a DIY approach marked by a parallel anti-economic mandate, did not necessarily benefit financially or in terms of cultural prestige from its decisions.

Godard maintains that such differentials reflect the conditions of the "feminist sub-field" in the larger field of cultural production: "In a feminist sub-field . . . [the] same disinterestedness or anti-economic behaviour is unable to transpose its disavowal of short-term profit in the marketplace into long-term prestige in other fields."[89] Godard's analysis provides a plausible explanation for why Riot Grrrl has, unlike other "indie" creative movements that emerged in the early to mid 1990s, remained both unprofitable and largely unrecognized as an *artistic* and *literary* movement. What Godard's analysis fails to fully account for, however, is that the "feminist sub-field" is also a space of possibilities.

Far from preserving the history of Riot Grrrl as it has been preserved to date, the Riot Grrrl Collection represents a *possible* interruption in both the field of cultural production and its feminist subfield. Although the possibilities are, thus far, mostly unexplored, as researchers use the collection its possibilities will become increasingly apparent. As emphasized throughout this chapter, without necessarily pushing Riot Grrrl's status as a subculture or submovement of punk entirely into the background, the collection's location at Fales Library and Special Collections relocates Riot Grrrl in relation to some of the "rarefied" and "consecrated" cultural products of earlier and concurrent avantgarde literary, art, and performance movements, hence drawing attention to the fact that the "grrrls" *were* engaged in forms of cultural and knowledge production that can and should be taken seriously as art, literature, and theory and not simply youthful rebellion. The collection's development, which is the result of the longstanding relationship between the collection's archivist and donors, reveals the extent to which these cultural producers recognized the archive as the space and apparatus most capable of executing such a radical position-taking in the present.

4 /   Radical Catalogers and Accidental Archivists: The Barnard Zine Library

These days I see myself as somewhere between activism and scholarship. I am not as actively engaged as I once was in political demonstrations and campaigns, and I am not writing about them much either, not even on my blog. What I am doing . . . is collecting, preserving, and providing access to the creative, emotional, and intellectual output of young women activists, in the form of zines. It is not just my political orientation, however, that informs my work with zines; it is my librarian orientation: reference . . . whenever there is a choice to make, I tend to privilege access over preservation.

—JENNA FREEDMAN, "The Zines are in Charge:
A Radical Reference Librarian in the Archives,"
The Metropolitan Archivist

I met Jenna Freedman at Barnard College, the women's college at Columbia University, in 2006. On the occasion of my first visit, Freedman, perhaps more widely known as the "zine librarian" and sometimes simply as the "blue-haired librarian,"[1] gave me a tour of the zine library she founded at the Barnard Library in 2003. Later, we spent an hour or so talking about the collection and her thoughts on librarianship, archiving, feminism, and activism. As I was about to leave, she invited me to meet up with a group of librarians and her later that evening on the Lower East Side "by the Temperance Fountain in Tompkins Square Park—if it's raining, at the cafe across the street." It must have been raining because later that evening I found Freedman and a half dozen or so other librarians sprawled on a collection of sofas at a cafe across from the park. In contrast to the librarians and archivists I had come to know over the course of several previous research projects, this group was younger and

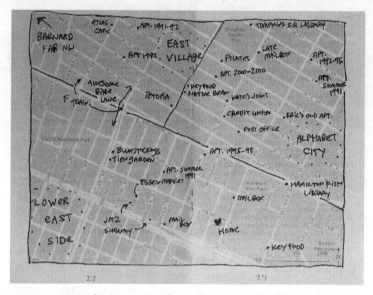

FIGURE 4.1 Map by Jenna Freedman. Featured in *Lower East Side Librarian Winter Solstice Shout Out 2010* (private collection of author), courtesy of Jenna Freedman.

more preoccupied with politics than preservation. As the meeting progressed, I learned that I had been invited to a meeting of the New York City chapter of Radical Reference—an activist librarian collective that had formed two years earlier to offer research support to demonstrators, activists, and the independent media during the Republican National Convention in New York. As expressed in their mandate: "Radical Reference is a collective of volunteer library workers who believe in social justice and equality [and] support activist communities, progressive organizations, and independent journalists by providing professional research support, education and access to information . . . in a collaborative virtual setting."[2] During the meeting, members talked about upcoming workshops and actions and about expanding their online presence. Following the meeting, Freedman invited me to join her at her final destination of the day—a party celebrating the resolution of the artist center/squat

ABC No Rio's historic fight to purchase 156 Rivington Street from the City of New York.[3] Along with most of the contingent from the Radical Reference meeting, we walked across Tompkins Square Park and down Avenue B to the corner of Clinton and Rivington. At ABC No Rio, young punk kids hung out with an eclectic mix of longstanding Lower East Side residents, including hundreds of housing rights activists, artists, writers, and musicians who had participated in ABC No Rio's history and drawn out struggle with the city. Not only did Freedman know many people at ABC No Rio that evening, but she also knew people from a surprising spectrum of backgrounds. She introduced me to a group of young volunteers from the ABC No Rio Zine Library—a community-based collection housing more than twelve thousand zines and independent magazines.[4] She introduced me to *New York Times* reporter Colin Moynihan, who was there as both a reporter and a local resident/supporter.[5] And she introduced me to her partner, housing and media activist Eric Goldhagen, who had played a role in spearheading the fight to purchase the ABC No Rio building from the city for a dollar. This, I discovered, was not only Freedman's neighborhood (for years, she has lived within a few blocks) but also the community of activists and cultural workers she calls home. On my initial visit to the Barnard Zine Library, I did much more than browse the shelves—I shadowed the "Lower East Side librarian" (Freedman's moniker and the title of her blog)[6] through a day in her life.

Notably Freedman's typical day spans at least two distinctly different urban spaces. As Barnard College advertises on its website, "Visitors are often surprised when they enter our historic gates and the sounds of the city melt away. Barnard's compact campus provides a serene respite, an oasis from the sometimes-frenetic energy of a city that never sleeps."[7] On Barnard's campus, gates are evidently designed to keep people in—namely the college's small, carefully selected cohort of young women. By contrast, in Freedman's neighborhood, gates, such as those surrounding Tompkins Square Park, are designed to keep people out, at least certain people at certain times of day.[8] I highlight Freedman's movement through some of New York's more notable gated spaces because her movement through these various gates is something she carries into all aspects of her work as a librarian and "accidental archivist" at Barnard College and in the eclectic communities of practice she traverses as a citizen and activist.[9] Across sites, Freedman is intent on finding creative ways to break down and open up the systems and grids that confine us to not only highly regulated urban geographies but also the knowledge networks we navigate on a day-to-day basis in our search for information. This is why she privileges not only "access over preservation," but also "anarcho-punk-influenced zine community mores, rather than the tenets of librarianship,"[10] at least when the two are in conflict. As I explore throughout this chapter, however, Freedman's project is not, as one might expect, about letting chaos reign in the library. As she explains, anarchism, in this context generally understood as "a way of life in favor of egalitarianism and environmentalism and against sexism, racism, and corporate domination,"[11] is important to most contemporary punks. At its core, she explains, "Being punk is a way of critiquing privileges and challenging social hierarchies."[12] Bringing an "anarcho-punk-influenced" philosophy to traditional practices of librarianship, including collecting and cataloging, then, is not about disregarding the necessity of order in either the library or the archive; rather, it is an attempt to alter the hierarchies that these spaces reify through their established practices of collecting and categorization. And this, I maintain, is how Freedman is altering the epistemic terrain in the present and the future for the girls, women, and gender-queer subjects who are the authors, distributors, and readers of the zines in her collection.

In this final case study, it is important to acknowledge that my focus is not an exclusively archival space. The Barnard Zine Library includes both an open stacks collection and an archival collection, and the collection's founder is a reference librarian who, by virtue of founding the collection, has become deeply engaged in the work of developing and theorizing special collections and archives. The fact that the Barnard Zine Library straddles the boundaries between collection and archive and that its founder persistently crosses professional boundaries—including those that typically separate reference librarians, special collections librarians, catalogers, archivists, and scholars—means that the collection in question has become a site of activism informed by archival principles but by no means structured by the constraints of more traditional archives, including those discussed in chapters 2 and 3.

The Making of a DIY Collection

The Barnard Zine Library began with an ambitious proposal and modest budget in 2003. Recognizing that zines are a "nontraditional medium and potentially a little scary to administrators,"[13] Freedman's initial proposal included a seven-page rationale, primarily aimed at persuading her dean that zines, specifically zines by girls and women, belong in university-based libraries and that a special collection of this nature was especially in keeping with Barnard College's history and mission:

> Although zines have been around for a long time, few libraries have yet to begin collecting and preserving them. This project will allow Barnard to provide catalog access to these important publications on an item level, something that is not being done systematically by any major library that catalogs with the Online Computer Library Center (OCLC), which includes virtually every academic and public library in the United States and 85 other countries. Zines are a rich and democratic form of self-expression that range from scholarly treatises on diverse issues to wildly creative artworks. The collection and preservation of these materials will provide both contemporary and future researchers a unique insight into today's feminist culture.[14]

From the onset, Freedman's intentions for the Barnard Zine Library were driven by at least two distinct objectives: one centered on collection, and the other centered on cataloging. Only later did Freedman recognize and openly admit that these objectives were by no means entirely compatible. "If I knew what I was doing," Freedman admits, "None of this would have happened, so it's a good thing I was a bit naïve!"[15] For people outside the profession, the happy accidents guiding Freedman's work may not be apparent, but inside the profession the Barnard Zine Library represents a strange hybrid straddling the special collection, archive, and cataloged library collection.

At the center of Freedman's original proposal was an intention to establish an open stacks collection of noncirculating zines. In the original proposal, however, Freedman also sought to collect and preserve "born-digital" zines or "e-zines" and to further explore the possibility of digitizing print zines whenever possible, emphasizing that "providing electronic access to print zines is important for research use as well as for preservation."[16] As the collection developed, however, Freedman abandoned her proposed digitization project. In lieu of digitization, she eventually established a parallel archival collection, which not only holds doubles of all the zines found in the open stacks collection but also hundreds of additional zines (many donated as part of larger zine collections by former zine producers, readers, and individual collectors seeking a permanent home for their collections).[17] Despite the fact that in many respects Freedman's proposed collection became more rather than less attentive to the preservation of printed materials as it developed and even found Freedman, a reference librarian, becoming an archivist "by accident," the collection's profile and significance remained contingent on the advancement of another aspect of the originally proposed digital mandate.

Beyond Freedman's proposal to digitize print zines, she proposed to catalog the zines collected with the goal of ensuring their visibility to not only Barnard Library users but also all users of WorldCat, the world's largest online public access catalog.[18] The decision to catalog the zines was driven by a recognition that cataloging would make zines increasingly accessible to users worldwide while simultaneously heightening the visibility of both zines and contemporary feminist discourses. As Freedman emphasizes, cataloging the zines was important for several reasons. First, cataloging would enable readers and scholars to encounter them "just as they would any other print, electronic, or media holdings as they searched the catalog."[19] In other words, cataloging the zines was a way to change the status of zines by effectively making these self-published works just as visible and retrievable as published materials in the library catalog. Second, the cataloging would enable the zines to be made available through interlibrary loans and therefore expand their potential readership. Finally, the cataloging was a way to further disseminate contemporary feminist materials not only within the Barnard College Library but also to worldwide library users: "For us the priority was achieving visibility for the materials, and the legitimacy their presence in WorldCat would bestow on them."[20]

From the onset, then, Freedman's project has been about collecting and preserving zines for use by Barnard College students, faculty, and visiting researchers and more ambitiously about rendering visible zines and, more specifically, the unique content of feminist zines within library catalogs well beyond the catalog connected to the local collection. To this extent, Freedman's initial proposal and ongoing project has targeted two interconnected sites of activism—the actual space of the library (and in this case, a connected archive) and the more conceptual space of the library catalog and its extended virtual networks. During the past decade, however, as the Barnard Zine Library has grown (there are now 1500 zines in an open stacks collection and more than 4000 zines in a connected archive, many still unprocessed),[21] her objective to render zines, as well as Riot Grrrl and third wave feminist discourses more visible has also expanded. In the conclusion to "Girl Zines in the Library," a 2009 article published in *Signs*, Freedman states that when she started the collection at Barnard College she sought to "expand the discourse of women's studies materials available in our academic community and to a greater extent, in the world."[22] Indeed, this is precisely what she has done. A researcher searching WorldCat for materials related to Riot Grrrl or third wave feminism, for example, will now discover hundreds of zines in addition to a limited number of printed collections and monographs on these subjects. Because the vast majority of Riot Grrrl and at least a significant proportion of third wave publications were self-published, the fact that these zines appear in World-Cat searches is by no means insignificant. In short, through her decision to provide detailed catalog descriptions for all the zines in her collection Freedman has effectively accomplished access to a discourse on feminism that, at least until the late 1990s, was still primarily accessible only in private collections rather than in libraries around the world. In this respect, even more so than the zine collections housed at the Sallie Bingham Center or the papers housed in the Riot Grrrl Collection at NYU, the Barnard Zine Library has changed the visibility and arguably the status of the materials it houses and the discourses these documents contain. It is essential to bear in mind that for many zinesters the idea that to gain legitimacy zines must be housed in a library or an archive is itself a highly controversial statement. Nevertheless, it is difficult to deny the fact that for many readers outside the zine community, the presence of a zine title in the library and library catalog does matter.

Despite the fact that this chapter, more than any other chapters in this book, is as much the story of a collection as it is the story of an individual librarian and accidental archivist, it is important to note that the Barnard Zine Library is by no means driven solely by Freedman. As the director of research and instructional services at the Barnard College Library, zines are only a small part of her job. Although Freedman oversees the cataloging of zines, a large percentage of the catalog descriptions are produced by student assistants. More importantly, as part of Freedman's commitment to the communities of practice in which she is engaged, she has gone to great lengths to ensure that her university-based collection remains as community oriented and collaborative as possible.

Indeed, the collection is deeply inflected by the needs and desires of the zine producers with whom Freedman, a zinester herself, has developed longstanding relationships:

The fact that I am part of the community matters. I don't think that any of the other zines being catalogued are being catalogued by people who really get zines, who are involved in the making and reading of zines. After all, you can catalogue something without reading it. So unlike other people who are doing this work, they can't bring what I bring, because I am in the zine community.[23]

On at least two occasions, Freedman's dialogues with the community in question have even resulted in changes to the collection's mandate.

As part of Freedman's mandate to catalog all the zines in the Barnard Zine Library, whenever possible, zine producers' names are included in catalog descriptions. As a highly idiosyncratic form of publication, however, the inclusion of zine producers' names is neither always possible nor desirable. Often it is only possible to identify a zine producer's first name or pseudonym; moreover, a small number of zine producers feel uncomfortable with their names being linked to their zines in the library catalog. Such responses, while extremely rare, are by no means surprising. As discussed in chapter 2, girl zines often contain highly personal narratives and are typically produced in small print runs of fifty to one hundred for a semipublic textual community not for the vast community of readers who can access materials via interlibrary catalogs such as WorldCat. In contrast to most catalogers, then, Freedman maintains that, as part of her collaborative ethic, it is important to remain responsive to zine producers who wish to detach themselves from their publications. As Freedman explains, "Because I am in the zine community and I care so much about what people think and about how they feel about me and the collection, I make different decisions. Someone recently asked me to take her name out the catalog and I did. I didn't ask any questions. I just did it."[24]

Another change Freedman has made to her collection's mandate was developed to respond to the needs of transgender-identified zine producers. As Freedman explains, "we have a policy to ask people whose gender expressions have changed since they published their zine whether they feel comfortable having their work in a collection of women's zines."[25] Freedman's attempts to ensure that transgender zinesters are appropriately represented in the collection have been directly informed by outreach to both the zine and transgender communities. She explains:

> I started by presenting the old statement and a new version and soliciting feedback on our *LiveJournal* blog . . . Some back-and-forth on and off the website led us to our current statement. Community contributions were both surprising and helpful. We learned that in going out of our way to include trans women, we were actually reinforcing a difference. We might have done better to leave the statement as it was, at least regarding women (cis- and trans).[26]

Although Freedman admits that "getting e-schooled by the trans community was sometimes painful," she emphasizes that "it was educational and worth the effort" and believes that it will "yield trust dividends down the line," which she considers essential to building a collection that is truly collaborative and attentive to community needs.[27]

Alongside Freedman's ongoing work developing the Barnard Zine Library, during the past decade, she also established herself as librarian-scholar. Beyond presenting on various topics related to zine librarianship, activist librarianship, and the development of feminist collections at annual meetings of the American Library Association and conferences in other interdisciplinary fields ranging from gender studies to book history, Freedman regularly publishes articles about her collection and broader work as a feminist activist librarian in DIY publications, including her own zine, professional magazines, and refereed journals. Despite her visibility as a librarian-scholar, her approach remains deeply guided by her commitment to grassroots activism, punk, and the everyday realities of working as a reference librarian in a predominantly undergraduate library. In an article prepared for a feature on activism in the *Metropolitan Archivist* (originally prepared as a presentation to the School of Communication and Information at Rutgers University), for example, Freedman anticipates and addresses her readers' reaction to her colloquial style of presentation:

> You may be annoyed by the first person, casual tone of this presentation/essay. In part, the style is meant to mimic that of a personal zine. . . . The other part is to signal that the lines in my life as a librarian, an activist, and just me are extremely blurry. Many librarians identify strongly with their jobs, and I am no exception. I do a lot of Barnard work from home, and occasionally I do work for Radical Reference (a group of librarians who serve the information needs of activists and independent journalists) from Barnard. I feel like I am always "on" as a zine librarian, a member of Radical Reference, or as a librarian in general.[28]

As much as Freedman and her work are influenced by punk and by Riot Grrrl and third wave feminism, however, she is also the daughter of earlier generations of radical librarians. Although her tactical interventions into the library and archive are structured by relatively new technologies, including interlibrary databases such as WorldCat and social media tools ranging from blogs to Facebook, her activism extends an approach to collecting, cataloging, and preservation that emerged in the wake of 1960s countercultures and radical social movements.

Legacies of Radical Cataloging

Two years after my initial meeting with Jenna Freedman, I returned to New York, not as a visiting researcher but as a resident. Shortly after my arrival, Freedman invited me to join her for a Critical Mass ride. One of the many activist initiatives with which Freedman is associated, Critical Mass is best known for holding leaderless, consensus-driven bike rides through major urban centers around the world on the last Friday of every month.[29] On this occasion, the ride started at Union Square Park and moved through the streets of the East Village to Washington Square and then straight up the middle of 7th Avenue to Times Square. By the end of the ride, I had seen the city from a myriad of new vantage points, including perspectives usually available only to people moving through the city by car or bus. This being my first Critical Mass rally, however, I was also struck by the event's organization—close to one hundred cyclists of varying ages, genders, and ethnic and racial backgrounds moving by consensus *en masse* through New York, often straight up the middle of streets, sometimes against the flow of traffic, but entirely without incident. Critical Mass demonstrates that opening up new routes through the city does not necessarily require one to dismantle existing systems. At the center of Critical Mass is the very simple recognition that new avenues through which to experience and understand familiar spaces are always already available to anyone willing to move differently (not necessarily defiantly) through the grid.

Opening up new avenues of access is also the objective of radical librarians. However committed they are to working within existing structures and systems, radical librarians are also committed to opening up new routes through which to enter fixed structures. And like Critical Mass, they appreciate that new routes hold the potential to open up previously inaccessible perspectives and knowledges. But in the case of radical librarians, the target is not the space of the city but rather what feminist librarian, activist, and scholar Emily Drabinski describes as the library's "highly classified space" that reflects "an intellectual framework that is inhospitable to certain kinds of knowledges," including those that challenge traditional assumptions about gender and sexuality.[30] Like the city's grid, however, the highly classified space of the library is by no means entirely resistant to change. Indeed, its constraints are also sites of resistance, and nowhere is this more apparent than at the level of the library catalog itself.

One of the most widely used library classification systems in the world and the primary target of contemporary radical catalogers is the Library of Congress Classification (LCC) system. In contrast to other popular systems, relationships among topics in the LCC system are not indicated by an assigned number but rather by indenting subtopics under the larger topics of which they are part. In addition to being classified under one of the LCC's twenty-one basic classes (for example, B – Philosophy. Psychology. Religion, or J – Political Science), each entry is further divided into subclasses, and each subclass includes "a loosely hierarchical arrangement of the topics pertinent to the subclass, going from the general to the more specific."[31] Individual topics, therefore, may be further broken down by place, period, genre, or form.[32] The LCC system offers catalogers more opportunities to highlight the specificity of texts, yet the system itself reflects a desire to bring conformity to classification systems across the United States. As Melvil Dewey reflected during an American Library Association conference in 1896, "we shall never accomplish our best results in librarianship until we have at the National Library in Washington a center to which the libraries of the whole country can turn for inspiration, guidance, and practical help, which can be rendered so economically and efficiently in no other possible way."[33] Always erring on the side of efficiency, Dewey further observed, "If a book is published that 500 of these libraries will buy, where can you think of a greater waste than that every one of the 500 should have to undertake, each for itself, with, in most cases, limited bibliographic machinery and insufficient force, to catalog that book when it has been already cataloged in the National Library by the most expert staff in the country, having at their disposal every known resource?"[34] In short, Dewey believed that a central service cataloging books would be not only more efficient but also better positioned to render the nation's knowledge resources visible. As with any rational system, however, the development of the LCC system was contingent on ignoring or at least obscuring certain knowledges—namely, knowledges that emanate from the margin rather than the center. For this reason, despite the system's capacity to highlight the specificity of texts, over time, it has also entrenched a dominant standpoint, which is precisely the target of radical librarians and more precisely radical catalogers today.

There have likely been renegade catalogers since the introduction of Library of Congress subject headings (catalogers quietly making decisions that unsettle rather than reify social and political norms), but discourses on activist cataloging did not emerge until the late 1960s. At this time, the *ALA Bulletin* started to regularly publish short letters to the editor from Sanford Berman. At the time, Berman was an assistant librarian at the University of Zambia. Indeed, his location initially prompted him to think more seriously about the relationship between LC subject headings and social justice issues as he began to understand how racial epithets, such as *kaffir* (a South African term with the same resonance as the term *nigger* in the United States), had worked their way into the LCC system while other terms, which might render traditionally marginalized groups from African Americans to gays to the disabled more visible or visible on less discriminatory terms, had been routinely excluded. In 1971, Berman published his first of several books on radical cataloging, *Prejudices and Antipathies: A Tract on the LC Subject Heads Concerning People*. On the value of LC subject headings, Berman maintained, "There can be no quarrel about the practical necessity for such a labor-saving, worry-reducing work, nor—abstractly—about its value as a global standardizing agent, a means for achieving some uniformity in an area that would otherwise be chaotic."[35] However, the functionality of the LCC system has never been Berman's target; rather, from his earliest letter campaigns in the *ALA Bulletin*, his target has been the system's impact on real people and their lives:

> A subject-scheme should, ideally, manage to encompass all the facets of what has been printed and subsequently

collected in libraries to the satisfaction of the worldwide reading community. Should, that is. But in the realm of headings that deal with people and cultures—in short, with humanity—the LC list can only "satisfy" parochial, jingoistic Europeans and North Americans, white-hued, at least nominally Christian (and preferably Protestant) in faith, comfortably situated in the middle- and higher-income brackets, largely domiciled in suburbia, fundamentally loyal to the Established Order, and heavily imbued with the transcendent, incomparable glory of Western civilization. Further, it reflects a host of untenable—indeed, obsolete and arrogant—assumptions with respect to young people and women. And exudes something less than sympathy or even fairness toward organized labor and the sexually unorthodox or "avant-garde."[36]

For Berman, the LCC, which had become deeply static by the late 1960s when his campaign first appeared, was a system with great potential to be living, changing, and dynamic. He passionately argues this point in the introduction to *Prejudices and Antipathies*: "Just because the scheme germinated, historically, within a Western framework of late Victorianism, rampant industrial expansion, and feverish empire-building . . . just because, in short, we were 'brought up that way' is no valid reason for perpetuating, either in our crania or catalogs, the humanity-degrading, intellect-constricting rubbish that litters the LC list."[37]

From the onset, radical cataloging has been concerned with changing the terms used to include/exclude not only visible, ethnic, and linguistic minorities but also women, gays and lesbians, and children and youth while simultaneously working to introduce a lexicon that can account for new political and cultural movements. In the early 1970s, for example, the LCC system included a subheading for "WOMAN—RIGHTS OF WOMEN," but, as Berman argued at the time, in light of the emerging feminist movement the subhead was no longer adequate. "It might not easily have been foreseen in 1966," he observed, "But there has since arisen a vocal and powerful movement among women that transcends in its spirit and approach the conventional 'feminist' demands or agitation for 'rights.'"[38] Berman's "remedy" was to add a new subhead—LIBERATION—or introduce another entry, WOMEN'S LIBERATION MOVEMENT.[39] Along with his expressed concern about the depiction of racial minorities and women, in the early 1970s he also noted that it was imperative that "Homosexuality" and "Lesbianism" be removed from the prime heading of SEXUAL PERVERSION in light of the recognition that "the referent thus smears and blemishes a large and already much-harassed body of men and women, whose habits may be different, but not therefore more dangerous, disagreeable, or censurable, than those of the heterosexual majority."[40] In addition to his progressive interventions on racial, gender, and sexual minority rights, Berman's inaugural treatise on cataloging called for a rethinking of underground literature and the underground press because, as he astutely observed, "the 'underground literature' treated by the referred-to head is not the variously ribald, revolutionary, pro-pot, hard-rock, anti-Establishment, psychedelic, 'hip,' four-letter-word-larded produce of magazines and tabloids like *Oz, Georgia Straight, Great speckled bird, Los Angeles free press, IT, Avatar, Kaleidoscope*, and the *East Village Other*."[41] In this case, he proposed the introduction of UNDERGROUND PRESS,[42] subsequently heightening the visibility of alternative publications in the library catalog—a project that remains of great importance to Freedman in her ongoing effort to raise the visibility of zines.

While Berman's interventions are arguably the most well-known attempts to radicalize LC subject headings, simultaneous to his interventions, feminist librarians were actively organizing for change on a myriad of fronts from the catalog to the structure of the American Library Association and other professional organizations. The first feminist ALA task force emerged in the late 1960s when a group of women marching with the Librarians for Peace Brigade in Washington was prompted to reflect on their own rights within the workplace and society. The women subsequently formed the National Women's Liberation Front for Librarians (NWLFFL). Soon, the NWLFFL realized the need to think about women's liberation within their own profession, and by 1970 the group organized as a formal task force. In addition to tackling workplace inequities, the Task Force on the Status of Women turned its attention to the systematic ways in which the profession's practices—especially cataloging—continued to perpetuate sexism through the use of established Library of Congress subject headings.[43] In an optimistically titled article published in the *American Librarian*, "The Woman Arisen," Patricia Glass Schuman and Kathleen Weibel recount, "In 1974 the Task Force organized a Committee on Sexism in Subject Headings, which was influential in changing some LC topic headings. Recognizing that the changes were not far-reaching and that the problem of bias encompassed more than sex, the committee developed principles for establishing nonbiased subject headings for people and groups with common cultures."[44] Following the Task Force's initial interventions, cataloger Joan Marshall extended the committee's mandate by developing a thesaurus of indexing terms for materials on women. In the introduction to the resulting book, *On Equal Terms: A Thesaurus for Nonsexist Indexing and Cataloging,* Marshall takes on both sexist language and the LCC system's adoption of such language:

> Prescriptive grammarians have required the use of male sex-linked words to describe all the humankind. These words conceptually exclude women and impede the development in women of a positive self-image and thereby limit her conception of her role in society. If man is the norm, woman becomes the other.[45]

Marshall outlines a series of basic principles in cataloging designed to shift the terms through which women and other minorities are rendered visible in the library catalog. When possible, the "authentic name of ethnic, national, religious, social, or sexual groups should be established," or "if a group does not have an authentic name, the name preferred by the group should be established."[46] In addition, when establishing subdivisions, every effort should be made to "avoid words which connote inferiority or peculiarity."[47] As a rule, Marshall maintains that catalogers should avoid "value-loaded words" and "aim for neutrality."[48]

Without dismissing the importance of Marshall's contributions to feminist cataloging and more generally feminist librarianship, more than three decades after the publication of *On Equal Terms*, feminist librarians find themselves working in a transformed field. When Marshall published her treatise on nonsexist approaches to cataloging, the library catalog was still a set of cards housed in a cabinet—a system designed to help library patrons locate books on nearby shelves. Today, library catalogs are not only accessible from virtually any location in the world but invariably part of larger networks. As a result, a cataloger's work, whether they are working at a national library, is always already work destined to be visible well beyond their local context. At the same time, with the rise of catalog-informed social networking sites, such as LibraryThing, the function of the catalog continues to expand. As Bradley Dilger and William Thompson argue, in an age of integrated multifunction catalogs, "catalogs are not only the pathway to texts, but also a final destination."[49] As a site where information retrieval and social networking increasingly converge, the catalog has subsequently also gained import as a site of activism, which, however, is not the only thing that has changed since the publication of Marshall's treatise on cataloging.

During the past three decades, feminism itself has undergone a myriad of upheavals ranging from the identity politics debates that heightened awareness of the need to account for differences within the category of woman to the essentialism debates in feminist and queer theory that troubled identity categories altogether. When combined, these political and theoretical upheavals have rendered earlier feminist approaches to cataloging inadequately equipped to address contemporary feminist challenges. Indeed, where the category of woman is assumed to be an adequately inclusive category or where identity categories, such as woman, are assumed to have no genuine or authentic attributes, Marshall's call for catalogers to identify and adopt different groups' "authentic name" arguably runs counter to contemporary feminist politics and theorizing. If radical catalogers in the present differ from their predecessors, it is precisely on this basis. While using inclusive language and language preferred by the groups in question remains a guiding principle, radical catalogers are increasingly seeking to move beyond the goal of "neutrality."

Informed by a tradition of poststructuralist feminist theorizing on gender, Drabinski observes that "at the moment identity is fixed, it constitutes an unnamed excess, the 'stuff' of other ways of being that are not represented by . . . the named category."[50] But as she further observes, "The classification schemes that structure library space cannot account for this excess."[51] The project of contemporary radical catalogers, like Drabinski and Freedman, is to find ways to account for this excess, which is by no means an easy task. As Drabinski notes, "trans, tranny, trans dyke, MTF, M2F, FTM, F2M, genderqueer, femme, boi, butch, bear, aggressive, etc." may be terms that "represent shifting and overlapping sexual and gender identities," but in the library "books about these identities will be assigned static subject headings that collate sometimes widely divergent representations of gendered selves."[52] "These strange separations," Drabinski argues, "result from an intellectual framework that is inhospitable to certain kinds of knowledges, in this case those related to gender."[53] tatiana de la tierra makes a similar argument in her contribution to *Radical Cataloging: Essays at the Front:*

> While there is a diverse terminology for sexual identity,
> the Library of Congress distills it into variations of lesbian,
> gay, bisexual, and homosexual. Meanwhile, we are queers
> and queens, and transgender, and dykes, and bull daggers,
> and butches, and lipstick lesbians. We use code words: in

the life, familia. Latina lesbians are *mariconas, jotas, patas, tortilleras, areperas, patlache, gallonas,* and *cuaimas,* among other dazzling terms; most are derogatory words that were embraced after the fact.[54]

In contrast to earlier interventions in radical cataloging, such as those spearheaded by Marshall in the 1970s, de la tierra points out that in an attempt to avoid using once pejorative words, such as queer, the Library of Congress not only ignores the extent to which language, including identity categories, are fluid and historically and cultural contingent but also runs the risk of reifying hierarchies within marginalized groups. The risk is twofold: certain identities become less visible within the library catalog, even when they are present, and the knowledges connected to these identities invariably fall outside the intellectual framework produced by the space of the library. For this reason, it is no longer acceptable for radical catalogers to concentrate on purging the library catalog of pejorative words and labels and replacing them with less offensive terms. Building on the pioneering work of figures like Berman and Marshall, the challenge facing today's radical catalogers is to find increasingly innovative ways to work within the relatively inflexible library catalog, specifically the LCC system. Freedman's work as a special collections librarian and cataloger—once again, two professional identities that rarely, if ever, merge—is one example of how contemporary activist librarians are adopting and adapting the library catalog as a site of activism.

Collecting and Cataloging in the Barnard Zine Library

I have already compared radical catalogers to the cyclists who participate in monthly Critical Mass rides by emphasizing that the intent in both cases is to find innovative ways to create new avenues of access in otherwise rigid grids. When I shared this analogy with Freedman, she wondered, "I once was on a Critical Mass ride, and we all decided to take our bikes onto the subway . . . what would the cataloging analogy be for that?"[55]

Perhaps, the answer to this question lies in Freedman's own approach to cataloging and more generally librarianship. After all, like Critical Mass riders who take their bikes on the subway and subsequently become a parasitic presence on another mode of transportation beneath the streets, Freedman's work as a reference librarian, cataloger, accidental archivist, and librarian-scholar has frequently entailed adopting, adapting, and even coopting practices. If she were trained as an archivist, she likely would have never proposed to do item-level cataloging for her special collection. Likewise, if she were a trained cataloger, she may have thought twice about cataloging zines, which tend to blur the boundaries between serial, book, and unpublished documents. Yet, however unorthodox and surprising her approach to collecting and cataloging may be, her objectives are clear: to bring more attention in the library, the library catalog, and scholarship to hitherto underrepresented perspectives, identities, and knowledges found exclusively or primarily in zines, and this includes accommodating perspectives, identities, and knowledges that are by definition always already in flux. Although it is difficult to summarize the scope and range of Freedman's specific interventions, I attempt to map the impact some of her work as a renegade special collections librarian, cataloger, and archivist has had on the accessibility and visibility of contemporary feminist and queer knowledges, while paying specific attention to the impact of her efforts on the visibility of Riot Grrrl and third wave feminist activism and cultural and knowledge production.[56]

"Riot Grrrl Movement" first appeared as an official Library of Congress subject heading in the early 2000s, entering the Library of Congress printed edition of the "Red Book," which lists available subject headings, in 2002. In this case, the heading was proposed by a Library of Congress cataloger for Cherie Turner's book, *Everything You Need to Know About the Riot Grrrl Movement*.[57] While Riot Grrrl Movement exists as a subject heading, related categories such as Riot Grrrl Music and simply, Riot Grrrl, were never introduced. Despite the relative inflexibility of working with this single subject heading, its relatively early introduction meant that as Riot Grrrl related materials, including self-published materials, have migrated into the library, they have been cataloged as materials connected to the Riot Grrrl Movement as opposed to subsumed by less accurate subject headings.

Nevertheless, in the case of Riot Grrrl, the mere introduction of a subject heading would have been insufficient without the efforts of individual librarians, like Freedman. After all, a subject headings' impact is entirely contingent on the extent to which it is put into circulation. From the onset, Riot Grrrl was a movement committed to controlling its means of production at all cost, and, as a result, despite later efforts to anthologize some Riot Grrrl publications, the vast majority of the movement's publications took the form of self-published zines. In the course of my research, I discovered that a WorldCat search under the keyword "Riot Grrrl" yields 698 items; of the 698 items that appear, 311 are categorized as journals and magazines and only 266 as books. A closer examination of the results, however, reveals that among the 266 books there are several self-published zines, and of the 311 periodicals listed the vast majority are zines.[58] Searching through the results, Freedman's work as a collector and cataloger is readily apparent. More than 250 of the periodicals listed under the search term Riot Grrrl are available in the Columbia University Libraries system, and most notably, with few exceptions, the only zines that appear with searchable abstracts, table of contents, and Library of Congress subject headings are those housed in the Columbia University Libraries system.[59] In other words, without Freedman's initiative to both collect and catalog zines not only would the majority of Riot Grrrl publications be unavailable as potential research resources in library catalogs worldwide, but also and more significantly the content of the zines would be unsearchable. As a result of Freedman's cataloging initiative, it is possible to carry out research on a wide range of Riot Grrrl related subjects not only from within the Columbia University Libraries system but also from libraries around the world. In short, if it were not for the Barnard Zine

Library and Freedman's decision to carry out item-level cataloging for the zines in the collection, a search under the keyword "Riot Grrrl" in WorldCat would yield substantially fewer documents; that is, Riot Grrrl materials would simply be less visible and accessible to researchers worldwide.

Beyond facilitating research on the Riot Grrrl movement, Freedman's efforts have changed what aspects of feminism in the 1990s and beyond are rendered visible in the library catalog. For example, a search in WorldCat for materials published in 1995 under the very broad term "feminism" brought up not only books published that year, including Rebecca Walker's edited collection, *To be Real: Telling the Truth and Changing the Face of Feminism*, which contains a foreword by Gloria Steinem and afterword by Angela Davis, but also zines published in print runs as small as a few dozen copies, such as *Terrorist* by Rita Brinkerhoff, which is described in the abstract on the Columbia University Library website as a zine by an author "in her late teens" who is "a queer art school drop out in the Kansas punk and goth scene."[60] Because books like *To be Real* appear in the library catalog alongside zines like *Fucktooth, Cupzize, Race Revolt, The I in Feminism, Hoax,* and *Fusion: a zine by the original outcast,* researchers now have access to not only the feminist discourses circulating in the academy and popular media since 1990 but also discourses that were not part of a highly publicized dialogue on feminism during the past two decades. In *Fusion*, a personal zine or perzine by Meena Ramakrishnan, the reader encounters a young immigrant woman's perspective on women's oppression and social hierarchies and sexism in high schools. In *The I in Feminism*, a Rutgers College student and member of the campus group the Radigals reflects on her relationship with feminism and ability to incorporate it into a discussion of race and class. In *Cupzize*, two young women, one a graduate of Barnard, reflect on politics, music, feminism, and bisexuality. In *Race Revolt*, British zinesters reflect on race relations and whiteness within radical communities, queer issues, and feminism. On their own, a zine like *Figure 8*, which grapples with sizism, or

Feminist Economics: How the Man Tries to Keep us Down, which tackles the relationship between race, class, gender, and subjects ranging from neoliberalism to alternative economies, may not be significant, but collectively their visibility in library catalogs cannot be ignored. The presence of self-published feminist materials in this context ensures that Riot Grrrl writing—not simply writing about Riot Grrrl (for example, this book and other scholarly reflections on the subject)—is available in research documents and not simply in archival ephemera, which, however important, is generally less likely to be accessed because archival materials are also less likely to be item-level cataloged.

It is important to emphasize, however, that Freedman's collection at Barnard College has never been an exclusively Riot Grrrl collection. Indeed, one way in which she distinguishes her collection from aligned collections, such as the Riot Grrrl Collection at NYU, is by emphasizing the fact that her focus is zines and not simply those connected to the Riot Grrrl movement but zines produced by the "every grrrl,"[61] including girls who never identified with Riot Grrrl. For this reason, Freedman has also sought to introduce other Library of Congress subject headings that might help to make contemporary feminist materials more visible and searchable. Most notably, she played an integral role in introducing what she describes as the "—wave feminisms."

The lobby, first articulated in Freedman's annual zine, *The Lower East Side Librarian Winter Solstice Shout Out*, and on her much more frequently published blog, *The Lower East Side Librarian*, called for the introduction of a set of subject headings that would enable catalogers to identify materials using the terms First-Wave, Second-Wave, or Third-Wave Feminism or Feminists.[62] Despite the fact that gender studies scholars since the 1960s have relied on this wave metaphor as a means to demarcate different historical periods in feminism (for example, early twentieth-century suffrage activism or the 1960s to 1970s radical feminist activism), until 2008, the "waves" were not recognized as subject headings. For Freedman, the absence posed specific challenges because the mandate of her special collection

Lower East Side Librarian
Reading Log 2010

IMAGE from a T-shirt seen at the Fanzipothèque in Poitiers, France

FIGURE 4.2 Cover of *Lower East Side Librarian Reading Log 2010* (private collection of author), courtesy of Jenna Freedman.

is to collect third wave feminist zines, which may or may not be
Riot Grrrl related and may or may not hold anything in common
with what we readily imagine as second wave feminist materials.
In response to Freedman's lobby, which was subsequently taken
up by veteran catalogers and catalog activists, including Berman, the Library of Congress introduced Third Wave Feminism
along with First Wave Feminism and Second Wave Feminism,
providing the following definitions:

150 FIRST-WAVE FEMINISM

680 Here are entered works on the feminist movement of
the nineteenth and early twentieth centuries that focused
on reform of women's social and legal inequalities, especially on the gaining of women's suffrage.

150 SECOND-WAVE FEMINISM

680 Here are entered works on the period of feminist
thought and activity that began in the 1960s and focused
on economic and social equality for women, and on the
rights of female minorities.

150 THIRD-WAVE FEMINISM

680 Here are entered works on the period of feminist
thought and activity that began in the 1990s and focused
on expanding the common definitions of gender and sexuality by encompassing such additional themes as queer theory, transgender politics, womanism, ecofeminism, liber-
tarian feminism, etc.[63]

In this context Freedman's work as a librarian and cataloger may
appear to come into conflict with the positions adopted by many
feminist theorists of her generation. The wave analogy, after all,
runs the risk of reifying particular narratives about feminism that
fail to account for both the specificity and complexity of feminist activism across cultures and over time. In short, the waves
analogy is arguably part of what is wrong with Western feminist

storytelling—a trope that continues to hamper feminist theory's attempt to, as Clare Hemmings argues, tell stories differently.[64] But this is where the work of librarians and archivists arguably differs most notably from the work of scholars. Relishing ambiguities, after all, is much more possible and desirable for those of us who theorize feminism than for our colleagues charged with the task of making feminist knowledges retrievable in the increasingly complex information networks where knowledges circulate. It is important to further note that despite the fact that librarians, especially those engaged in the meticulous but necessary labor of cataloging, may appear intent on reifying categories, radical catalogers are also working to crack open identitarian categories.

The Library of Congress's articulated rationale for adopting the term third wave feminism states that the third wave has expanded "the common definitions of gender and sexuality by encompassing such additional themes as queer theory [and] transgender politics." Ironically, however, queer is not recognized as a LCC subject heading. As a result, zines, such as *Queer Ramblings*—a compilation zine intent on "getting rid of the gender binary" and featuring articles on "female-to-male transitions, using gender neutral terms, and being a 'straight butch'"— continues to be cataloged under the somewhat erroneous LCC subject headings of "Lesbians' writings—Periodicals; Lesbians—Poetry—Periodicals; Lesbianism in art—Periodicals" and even "Homosexuality—Periodicals."[65] Because the zine is explicitly queer rather than lesbian or homosexual, the subject headings arguably undermine the publication's mandate and misrepresent its content. This is significantly another one of Freedman's Library of Congress subject heading targets: "The lack of an access point for people who identify as queer, rather than gay, lesbian, or bisexual," she maintains, is a problem because "the umbrella term available for queer is 'sexual minorities,' which is not especially popular with those whom it is meant to describe."[66] In addition, Freedman recognizes that the political and theoretical connotations of queer are, inside and outside the queer community, entirely different from the political and theoretical connotations of terms such as gay, lesbian, and homosexual. Finally, queer connotes much more than a sexual orientation. Broadly defined, the term queer has come to be understood as a political and theoretical orientation that pushes against normative logics of all kinds. This is precisely the sort of ambiguity that the library catalog struggles to accommodate. If Freedman is especially concerned with lobbying for the inclusion of new subject headings, such as queer, it partly reflects the fact that identity categories are at the center of her cataloging agenda because, as she explains, in the case of zines, cataloging often begins with the identity of the zine producer, given the "subject content is not consistent enough to warrant LC or other subject shelving in our current collection."[67] The challenge of focusing on authors rather than the content of zines, however, is that authors are also subject to change (for example, an author may publish a zine as a woman but later become male-identified).

Although there is no denying the fact that the library represents "an inescapable constriction," there are always ways to at least push up against the constrictions of the space in order to engage in the work of "troubling knowledge organization as objective, apolitical, and value-free, and in creating library space that facilitates movement through the collection in ways that encourage the generation of new and unlikely knowledge formations."[68] The Barnard Zine Library—by most standards, a relatively small collection— exemplifies how one might carry out this work. Freedman, after all, continues to find innovative ways to expose not only the limits of established systems of information storage and retrieval but also to pry open their potential to accommodate knowledges that have historically remained invisible or at least obscured.

Imagining Possible Worlds

Each case study in this book has considered how archives and special collections have become increasingly integral to a feminist project equally committed to legitimizing knowledges and forms of cultural production that may otherwise be dismissed and imagining other ways to be in the world at a moment when the political and economic situation continues to erode our ability to imagine radical alternatives. These spaces of collection, preservation, and order are also spaces integral to imagining possible worlds. As I have argued throughout this book, without compromising their allegiance to history, these collections are also deeply oriented to the future.

It is instructive to return to the curious introduction that opens Michel Foucault's *The Order of Things*. The book, he claims, "first arose out of a passage in Borges, out of the laughter that shattered, as I read the passage, all the familiar landmarks of my thought—*our* thought . . ."[69] The memorable passage in question cites "a certain Chinese encyclopedia" that divides animals into a series of seemingly unfathomable categories that range from "belonging to the Emperor" and "embalmed" to "sucking pigs" and "sirens" to "frenzied" and "innumerable" and so the list continues. As Foucault observes, "In the wonderment of this taxonomy, the thing we apprehend in one great leap . . . is the limitation of our own, the stark impossibility of thinking *that*."[70] But as he continues, "what is it impossible to think, and what kind of impossibility are we faced with here?"[71] Foucault's point, made via Borges, is simple: the order of things is as grounded in flights of fancy, imaginary worlds, and utopian projections as it is in logic. Foucault further reflects, "Order is, at one and the same time, that which is given in things as their inner law, the hidden network that determines the way they confront one another, and also that which has no existence except in the grid created by a glance, an examination, a language."[72] Order, in this view, is both deeply essential and essentially fabricated. Order is both that which one cannot escape and that which enables us to imagine possible worlds. Purely restrictive and purely speculative, the order of things is everything that holds us back and everything that enables us to be liberated from established constraints. Understood along these lines, order is not opposed to resistance but always already what might make the rejection of existing systems of thought and established grids of intelligibility possible. As a result, order is precisely what structures resistance from start to finish.

While there are no sucking pigs in Freedman's catalog, there are sirens and a myriad of other fanciful divergences. Freedman has not created a taxonomy as idiosyncratic as the titles and topics featured in many zines, but her decision to collect zines at the Barnard College Library, which is part of the Columbia University Libraries system, and to further catalog the zines in WorldCat challenges us to face the limitations of our own thinking. Her project, after all, is not simply about preserving the work of a specific cross-section of underrepresented subjects but more importantly about opening up ways to imagine being in the world differently.

Donna Haraway's nearly thirty-year-old manifesto on cyborgs tellingly concludes with a discussion of "phallogocentric origin stories," or those stories built into the "literal technologies—technologies that write the world, biotechnology and microelectronics—that have recently textualized our bodies as code problems on the grid of C^3I."[73] In the 1980s, Haraway predicted that in the late twentieth century and beyond, "feminist cyborg stories," which include a range of discursive interventions, will "have the task of recoding communication and intelligence to subvert command and control."[74] Significantly, she presents the cyborg as both a trickster and a coder—a being equally attentive to the work of subversion and inscription. Radical librarians like Freedman are doing precisely this work—recoding communication and intelligence so previously unimaginable identities, including genders and sexual orientations that resist the prevailing binary code, can become visible. In this sense, the seemingly banal work of collecting marginal texts and cataloging them is significant to the extent that it becomes part of a larger epistemological project. "The project of remapping the epistemic terrain," argues Lorraine Code, "is subversive, even anarchistic, in challenging and seeking to displace some of the most sacred principles of standard Anglo-American epistemologies."[75] As tricksters and coders, radical librarians and catalogers are engaged in the work of reinscribing the epistemic terrain by situating knowers in spaces that were previously inaccessible and rendering certain knowers visible where previously obscured. Without downplaying the importance of digital archives, I maintain that the cataloging work of activist librarians like Jenna Freedman cannot be underestimated. Indeed, her cataloging project demonstrates that the act of reinscription (tagging) may hold even greater potential for social change than the act of media transfer (digitization).

Conclusion

Outrage in Order

In many respects, this book opens where Ann Cvetkovich's *An Archive of Feelings* ends. Although Cvetkovich's study is concerned with queer and lesbian archives rather than feminist archives, the overlaps between our studies are notable; at times they cover similar terrain and even refer to some of the same collections, cultural phenomena, and urban geographies. Yet, as I emphasized throughout this book, much has changed since the publication of Cvetkovich's book more than a decade ago. In 2003, the archives of women born during and after the rise of the second wave feminist movement were still largely found in cultural products of our own making (zines, films, photographs, and private and eclectic collections). In 2013 much of this material has migrated to institutional archives, including university-based collections. This trend was evidently already apparent to Cvetkovich as she finished writing her book in the early years of the new millennium. She cautions in the concluding chapter: "as more institutionalized archives develop gay and lesbian collections, it will be increasingly important not to forget the more queer collection and strategies of the grassroots archives."[1] What she anticipated or intuited is the growth of queer and feminist archives in institutional spaces that may or may not honor the legacies of community-based and volunteer-run collections, including institutions like the Lesbian Herstory Archives. On this account, Cvetkovich further wondered, "Will the two kinds of archives end up competing with one another?"[2]

In 2013, it is possible to conclude that the legitimate fear about the development of institutional collections imperiling the existence of community-based collections is largely unfounded. My own interviews with donors, archivists, librarians, and scholars suggest quite the opposite may hold true, at least in the case of archival collections with a mandate to collect materials related to feminist and queer women's histories of struggles. All the professional archivists and librarians I met during the course of researching this book also spend time working in communities; some give talks and workshops related to their respective collections, and others share their time and professional expertise with community-based collections. In addition, the archivists and the librarians I met are aware of and attentive to the importance of noninstitutional archives, such as the Lesbian Herstory Archives. The archivists and librarians I encountered while researching and writing *The Archival Turn in Feminism* consistently maintained that what they are doing complements but by no means competes with the work of community-based archives. Freedman, for example, expresses her gratitude to librarians and archivists, professional and DIY, who are creating digital zine archives, specifically citing the work of the Queer Zine Archive Project;[3] such initiatives take some pressure off her to respond to everyone's needs in the context of her collection and, more importantly, allow her to create another vital avenue of access to feminist and queer zines.[4] Similarly, in reference to the Riot Grrrl Collection at NYU, Darms explains, "I think what we offer is something that can't be offered in a DIY archive," but "I also think both things will continue to happen." As she emphasizes, "These are parallel projects."[5]

For this reason, rather than ask whether institutional collections will threaten the survival of collections that may be variously characterized as community-based, *ad hoc*, DIY, and queer, as I conclude this study, I am faced with a different set of questions than scholars, archivists, collectors, and activists faced in 2003. How might the process of putting our outrage in order—collecting and ordering the cultural and intellectual products of resistance movements—remain deeply attached to the communities of practice from which they emerge as they migrate to established archives? How might the archivization of activist movements in university-based collections, especially at privately funded institutions, continue be understood and experienced as parallel and even allied projects to community-based, volunteer-run, DIY initiatives? If activist-based collections housed in private university archives are in parasitic relation to their hosts, can they, over time, maintain such a relationship or will they eventually become inculcated by broader institutional mandates? What's at stake for knowledge production and activism when we foster these relationships?

I appreciate that some readers of this book may cynically conclude that the feminist collections at the center of this study have developed at private universities because we now live in an era when everything, even resistance, is becoming increasingly privatized. While this may be true (after all, it seems to be more than a coincidence that private universities appear better positioned than public universities to accommodate and support the development of these collections), I hope that among other things this study has foregrounded the fact the placing our outrage in order has always been a complex and contradictory endeavor. As discussed at length in chapter 1, for example, early feminist archival projects, such as the World Center for Women's Archives, may have been initiated by women with links to radical social movements and histories of direct action, but they were also reliant on the support of women with money, celebrity, and mainstream political clout. Similarly, in the 1970s, the political necessity to respond to women's needs in the present often meant that feminist collections, even those that claimed to have a mandate to collect and preserve historical documents, were often more concerned with disseminating contemporary information than with preservation. They were, quite literally, collections with contradictory temporal orientations—orientations that sometimes appeared to run in opposite directions. Running in opposite directions, however, has not necessarily resulted in the demise of these activist-oriented collections. Indeed, most of the collections discussed throughout this book, including those initiated during the decline of first wave feminist activism and the height of second wave feminist activism, have persisted in some way, shape, or form because of, not despite, their contradictory mandates and temporal orientations.

How best to archive radical movements and histories of struggle is, however, a question that is by no means easily resolved—something that became increasingly apparent as I was completing this book. Even before Occupy Wall Street had become the Occupy Movement, a group of librarian activists started to collect and catalog donated books at Zucotti Park. By the time the "People's Library" was confiscated by the New York City Police in an early morning raid on November 15, the library had grown to an estimated 3600 books and documents. Following the raid, major newspapers not only featured articles on the violence that had been unleashed on protesters but on the fate of the library, which had been reduced to a heap of mostly unsalvageable books and shipped to a Department of Sanitation facility in midtown Manhattan. Far fewer people realized that simultaneous to the development of the People's Library, a much smaller group of volunteers had intiated an archive. Spearheaded by a young part-time subject librarian at New York University, the Occupy Wall Street Archive began as a modest collection of posters and other ephemera. Within a few days, a working group had formed at Zucotti Park, and the group was carting away hundreds of posters and flyers daily. In contrast to the People's Library, the archive not only received less mainstream media attention and less support from within the Occupy Movement but also proved far more controversial and fraught. An online account by a member of the small working group overseeing the archive's development reveals that even within the working group, members held radically divergent positions on whether the archive should remain entirely renegade or align itself with an established collection, such as NYU's Tamiment Library & Robert F. Wagner Labor Archives, which formally reached out to the working group early in the archive's development. As Michelle Dean reflects in an account of the Occupy Wall Street Archive posted, less than a month after the raid of Zucotti Park: "The entire idea of institutional collaboration is a fraught one. On the one hand, it could open up a world of resources and money. On the other, the longer the group remains independent, the more control it can continue to have over the shape of the collection, and most importantly, future access to the materials."[6]

As I conclude this book and reflect upon this recent attempt to archive a radical movement as it unfolded, I wonder what, if anything, the activist archivists at Zucotti Park might have learned from the archives and special collections discussed in this book. On the surface, these collections housed in university libraries and archives may appear to share little in common with the random stashes of signs and printed ephemera that the working group members at Zucotti Park came to name as the Occupy Wall Street Archive. In reality, however, most of the collections at the center of this book had surprisingly similar origins. In the opening pages of *Girls to the Front*, Sara Marcus describes just such an archive, discovered in a punk activist house in the early 1990s when she was still searching for Riot Grrrl. "Beneath the staircase," she writes, "stood a shoulder-high metal filing cabinet that held relics of Riot Grrrl's history.... I found old meeting minutes, convention schedules, directories of chapters across the country.... I found pasted-up originals of old zines.... I found drawers stuffed full of letters from girls like me who had happened upon the address and written in, seeking encouragement, hope, connection."[7] Whether any of the contents of the filing cabinet from the punk activist house in Arlington ever found their way into the Riot Grrrl Collection or any of the other collections discussed in the preceding chapters of this book is unknown. We do know for certain that among the myriad of filing cabinets that filled up with lists of names and minutes from meetings and photographs and flyers and zines across North America throughout the 1990s, at least a few were recognized as potential materials for the archive, and along the way some of these materials found their way into institutional collections. However, it is important to bear in mind that simply collecting the documentary traces of an activist movement is not necessarily a subversive act.

What makes the archive a potential site of resistance is arguably not simply its mandate or its location but rather how it is deployed in the present. While archivists and special collections librarians play critical roles in fostering such possibilities, the onus is also on researchers working both inside and outside the academy to ensure that activist collections of all kinds continue to be *activated* in the present and for the future. Hence, I emphasize throughout this book the potentiality of the collections in question. At stake, then, are not the worlds these collections claim to represent, but rather the worlds they invite us to imagine and even realize.

NOTES

Introduction

1. Archiving Women, was promoted as "a one-day conference bringing together scholars and archivists to examine feminist practices in the archive" and sponsored by Columbia University's Center for Critical Analysis of Social Difference as part of the three-year project entitled, "Engendering the Archive, Toward an Intellectual History of Black Women." All references to the conference program in this discussion refer to the conference program posted at http://www.socialdifference.columbia.edu/events/archiving-women-conference

2. Jenna Freedman, "Archiving Women Report Back," *Lower East Side Librarian* (blog), February 2, 2009, http://lowereastsidelibrarian.info/reportback/ archivingwomen

3. Ibid.

4. Kelly, February 5, 2009 (11:40 a.m.), comment on Jenna Freedman, "Archiving Women Report Back," *Lower East Side Librarian*, February 2, 2009.

5. Emily, February 5, 2009 (12:28 p.m.), comment on Jenna Freedman, "Archiving Women Report Back," *Lower East Side Librarian*, February 2, 2009.

6. The preoccupation with the archive since the early 1990s is frequently described as the "archival turn." See, for example, Ann Laura Stoler's discussion in *Along the Archival Grain: Epistemic Anxieties and Colonial Common Sense* (Princeton, NJ: Princeton University Press, 2009), 44–46.

7. For a more detailed discussion of my observations at the Archiving Women symposium, see Kate Eichhorn, "D.I.Y. Collectors, Archiving Scholars and Activist Librarians." *Women's Studies: An Interdisciplinary Journal* 39 (2010): 622–646.

8. Astrid Henry, "Enviously Grateful, Gratefully Envious: The Dynamics of Generational Relationships in U.S. Feminism," *Women's Studies Quarterly* 34.3/4 (2006): 140–153.

9. For example, Ann Cvetkovich's *An Archive of Feelings* (Durham, NC: Duke University Press, 2003) and Judith Halberstam's discussion of queer subcultural archives in *In a Queer Time & Place* (Durham, NC: Duke University Press, 2005).

10. As noted in the preface, the original proposal for this book sought to trace the migration of Riot Grrrl and third wave feminist zines into a wide range of university, community, and activist archives. Over time, my focus both broadened to include materials beyond zines and narrowed to focus on university-based collections. Several readers of this manuscript have, not surprisingly, questioned the fact that in the process I have seemingly overlooked the role of digital archiving projects in the collection and preservation of feminist activism since the mid 1990s. While one cannot underestimate the importance of digitization initiatives undertaken by university and public collections and DIY archiving projects (i.e., QZAP, the Queer Zine Archiving Project), it is important to acknowledge that the collections at the center of this study—all focused on the collection and preservation of printed materials—emerged simultaneous to the spread of the web and reflected a conscious decision on the part of the archivists, librarians, and donors involved to privilege materiality over digitization. In addition, as I discuss at length in chapter 4 of this book, the decision to forego putting one's energy and resources into the creation of digital archives does not imply that these collections are averse to forms of new media activism. Indeed, all three collections have benefited from the widespread publicity available via the web, and in the case of the Barnard Zine Library, interlibrary online catalogs, such as WorldCat, have come to play a central role in the collection's visibility and impact beyond the collection's local origin.

11. While this may be a coincidence, it may also point to the fact that, in the United States, private institutions are paradoxically better positioned than public institutions to engage in collection development that represents some degree of political risk. This, however, is part of a larger discussion on the extent to which special collections are shaped by the mandates of funders, be they public or private.

12. Carolyn Steedman, *Dust: The Archive and Cultural History* (New Brunswick, NJ: Rutgers University Press, 2002), 1.

13. Cvetkovich, *Archive of Feelings*, 268.

14. Kate Eichhorn, "Archival Genres: Gathering Texts and Reading Spaces." *Invisible Culture*, 12 (Spring 2008) <http://www.rochester.edu/in_visible_culture/Issue_12/eichhorn/index.htm>.

15. David Harvey, "Neoliberalism and Creative Destruction," *Annals of the American Academy of Political and Social Science*, Vol. 610, NAFTA and

Beyond: Alternative Perspectives in the Study of Global Trade and Development (March 2007): 22.

16. Henry Giroux, "Terror of Neoliberalism: Rethinking the Significance of Cultural Politics." *College Literature* 32.1 (Winter 2005): 1–19.

17. Michel Foucault, *The Archaeology of Knowledge* (New York: Pantheon Books, 1972), 129.

18. Jacques Derrida, *Archive Fever: A Freudian Impression*, trans. Eric Prenowitz (Chicago: University of Chicago Press, 1996), 17.

19. Wendy Brown, *Politics Out of History* (Princeton: Princeton University Press, 2001), 95.

20. Ibid., 102.

21. Ibid., 113.

22. Michel Foucault, "Nietzsche, Genealogy, History," in *Language, Counter-Memory, Practice: Selected Essays and Interviews*, ed. Donald F. Bouchard (Ithaca, NY: Cornell University Press, 1977), 139.

23. Elizabeth Freeman, *Time Binds: Queer Temporalities, Queer Histories* (Durham: Duke University Press, 2010), xiv.

24. Ibid., xiii.

25. For more information, go to the New York Public Library Special Collections (http://www.nypl.org/archives/894) and to the ACT UP Oral History Project (http://www.actuporalhistory.org).

26. Colin Moynihan, "Homesteading a Little Place in History: Archive Documents Squatters' Movement on Lower East Side," New York Times, December 8, 2003, http://www.nytimes.com/2003/12/08/ nyregion/home-steading-little-place-history-archive-documents-squatters-move ment-lower.html?pagewanted=all&src=pm.

27. Harvey, "Neoliberalism," 2.

28. David Harvey, *Spaces of Neoliberalism: Towards a Theory of Uneven Geographical Development* (Stuttgart: Steiner, 2005), 72.

29. Barbara Godard, "Feminist Periodicals and the Production of Cultural Value: The Canadian Context," *Women's Studies International Forum* 25.2 (2002): 213.

30. This is not to imply that feminists were no longer publishing in the 1990s. Indeed, in the 1990s, many university presses had active series dedicated to the publication of feminist work. When I refer to the decline of the feminist publishing industry, I am referring specifically to the decline of women-owned publishing initiatives dedicated to publishing work "by women, for women."

31. Barbara Grier to Shameless Hussy Press, Shameless Hussy Press Records (Box 38, Misc. Business, 1986–1991), University of California Santa Cruz Special Collections and Archives.

32. Simone Murray, *Mixed Media: Feminist Presses and Publishing Politics* (London: Pluto Press, 2004), 9.

33. As Murray investigates in *Mixed Media*, while more mainstream women's presses, such as Virago Press and The Women's Press (both based

in the UK), survived and continued to flourish in the 1990s, the vast majority of women's presses, especially those with "women-only" policies and radical feminist convictions, had collapsed by the turn of the new millennium.

34. Murray, *Mixed Media*, 137.

35. Ibid., 127.

36. Trysh Travis, "The Women in Print Movement: History and Implications," *Book History* 11 (2008): 276.

37. Ibid., 295.

38. Murray, *Mixed Media*, 128.

39. Godard, "Feminist Periodicals," 221–222.

40. Murray, *Mixed Media*, 128–129.

41. On the surface, the perfect bound books produced by second wave feminist publishers and the zines produced by Riot Grrrls and third wave feminists may appear to share little in common. In reality, both second wave feminist books and Riot Grrrl and third wave feminist zines are the products of a mostly volunteer labor force, and both tend to be more focused on content than accuracy or precision. In addition, while zines are often distinguished from published books on the basis of the rich textual communities they foster, it is important to note that many early feminist publishers were also engaged in personal correspondence with their readers. At least in the late 1960s to the early 1970s, these publishers (i.e., Alta at Shameless Hussy Press) were still attempting to distribute feminist chapbooks and books without the support of established distribution networks or retailers.

42. Gail Chester, "The Anthology as a Medium for Feminist Debate," *Women's Studies International Forum* 25.2 (2002): 193–207.

43. Marlene Manoff notes that today, "Even librarians and archivists have become somewhat careless in their use of the term [archive]." See Manoff, "Theories of the Archive from Across the Disciplines," *Libraries and the Academy* 4.1 (2004): 10.

44. Foucault, *Archaeology of Knowledge*, 128.

45. Brown, *Politics*, 104.

46. Judith Halberstam, *Female Masculinity* (Durham: Duke University Press, 1998), 10.

47. Janice Radway, *Reading the Romance: Women, Patriarchy, and Popular Literature* (Chapel Hill: University of North Carolina Press, 1984).

48. Antoinette Burton, "Introduction: Archive Fever, Archive Stories," in *Archive Stories: Facts Fictions, and the Writing of History* (Durham: Duke University Press, 2005), 6.

49. John Ridener, *From Polders to Postmodernism: A Concise History of Archival Theory* (Duluth: Litwin Books, LLC), 105.

50. Cvetkovich, *Archive of Feelings*, 7.

51. Halberstam, *In a Queer Time & Place*, 170.

52. Ibid., 249.

53. Burton, "Introduction," 3.

54. Freeman, *Time Binds*, xvi.

1 / The "Scrap Heap" Reconsidered

1. Susan Faludi, "American Electra: Feminism's Ritual Matricide," *Harper's Magazine*, November 23, 2010, 40.

2. The No Longer in Exile Conference was hosted by the Gender Studies Program at The New School in March 2011. The complete schedule is available online at http://www.newschool.edu/lang/ academics.aspx?id=47785

3. Freeman, *Time Binds*, 62.

4. Ibid., 64–65.

5. Ibid., xiv.

6. Ibid., xvi.

7. Ibid., xiii.

8. Ibid, xiv.

9. Carolyn Dinshaw, *Getting Medieval: Sexualities and Communities, Pre- and Postmodern* (Durham: Duke University, 1999), 11.

10. Cvetkovich, *Archive of Feelings*, 242.

11. See, for example, Halberstam's discussion of queer archives in *In a Queer Time & Place*, 169–170.

12. "Archival genres" refer here to a range of texts, including scrapbooks, commonplace books, and zines, that privilege the collection and reordering of textual and visual materials as a composition practice. For more on "archival genres," see Eichhorn, "Archival Genres," in *Invisible Culture*.

13. Suzanne Hildenbrand, "Women's Collections Today," in *Women's Collections: Libraries, Archives, and Consciousness,* ed. Suzanne Hildenbrand (New York: Haworth Press, 1986), 2.

14. Ibid.

15. Anne Kimbell Relph, "The World Center for Women's Archives, 1935-–1940," *Signs* 4.3 (1979): 600.

16. Ibid., 601.

17. Hildebrand, "Women's Collections Today," 2.

18. Relph, "World Center," 599.

19. Ibid., 598.

20. World Center for Women's Archives (WCWA), Inc. *Brief report of World Center for Women's Archives* (Pamphlet) (November 13, 1939), 1.

21. Ibid., 1–2.

22. Relph, "World Center," 598.

23. Cited in Wolfgang Ernst, "Archival Action: The Archive as ROM and Its Political Instrumentalization under National Socialism," *History of Human Sciences* 12.2 (1999): 26.

24. Peter Fritzsche, "The Archive," *History & Memory* 17.1/2 (2005): 31.

25. Ibid.

26. Relph, "World Center," 599–600.

27. WCWA, *Brief report*, 2.

28. Francisca de Haan, "Getting to the Source: A 'Truly International' Archive for the Women's Movement (IAV, now IIAV): From its Foundation in Amsterdam in 1935 to the Return of its Looted Archives in 2003," *Journal of Women's History* 16. 4 (Winter 2004): 148.

29. Ibid., 149–152.

30. Appropriately, in 2009, on its 75th anniversary, the International Archive for the Women's Movement changed its name to Aletta, Institute for women's history, in recognition of its first donor, Aletta Jacobs.

31. de Haan, "Getting to the Source," 152.

32. Ibid., 153.

33. Ibid., 155.

34. Ibid., 156.

35. Relph, "World Center," 602.

36. Ibid., 603.

37. Anke Voss-Hubbard, "'No Document—No History': Mary Ritter Beard and the Early History of Women's Archives," *The American Archivist* 58.1 (Winter 1995): 22.

38. de Haan, "Getting to the Source," 156.

39. Ibid., 156–157.

40. Ibid., 157.

41. Ibid., 159.

42. Ibid., 162.

43. Ibid., 160.

44. Ibid., 162.

45. Ibid.

46. As Schwimmer emphasized in her introductory letter to potential donors in 1935, "The militarization of women is now progressing, expressed not only in the increased chauvinism of women's organizations, but literally (in the United States, for instance, the trend set in on May 27, 1929, when the Supreme Court decided that women are obliged to take up arms in defense of country)."

47. Eichhorn, "Archival Genres."

48. Hildenbrand, "Women's Collections Today," 137.

49. Ibid.

50. Ibid., 139.

51. Ibid.

52. Ibid.

53. Patricia Serafini, online interview, October 2011.

54. Hildenbrand, "Women's Collections Today," 145.

55. Cvetkovich, *Archive of Feelings*, 241.

56. The "History of Mandate" of the Lesbian Herstory Archives is published on the archive's website at http://www.lesbianherstoryarchives.org/history.html

57. Lauren Berlant, "'68, or Something," *Critical Inquiry* 21.1 (Autumn 1994): 125.

58. Ibid.
59. Ibid., 126.
60. Ibid.
61. Ibid., 127.
62. Freeman, *Time Binds*, 81.
63. Ibid., 82.

2 / Archives of Feminist Archiving

1. Clare Hemmings, *Why Stories Matter: The Political Grammar of Feminist Theory* (Durham: Duke University Press, 2010), 3.
2. Ibid., 149.
3. Shulamith Firestone and Anne Koedt, eds. *Notes from the Second Year: Women's Liberation: Major Writings of the Radical Feminists* (New York, 1970).
4. Joreen, "The Bitch Manifesto," in *Notes from the Second Year*, 5-8.
5. Riot Grrrlz Outer Space, *The Bitch Manifesto* (n.d.) (Sarah Dyer Collection, Duke University's David M. Rubenstein Rare Book & Manuscript Library).
6. As I was completing this book, I contacted Liz Henry (aka Lizzard Amazon) to ask permission to reprint the cover of her zine, and, as a result, I finally asked, "Did your message ever reach Freeman?" As it turned out, it did, seemingly long before I imagined it had. Henry confirmed, "I sent it to Jo Freeman many years ago, who said it was fine to reprint and pass out as a zine. It was amazing to write to her and get a real letter back! I didn't try to contact the editors. It didn't even occur to me (pre-web) when I printed the zine" (email to author, June 14, 2012). Henry's email confirmed, once again, that I had imagined most of the archive story in question.
7. The Sallie Bingham Center for Women's History and Culture opened in 1988 with a generous gift from writer, activist, and philanthropist Sallie Bingham. The gift was used to support the creation of a women's studies archivist position, charged with the task of collecting, cataloging, referencing, and promoting Duke University's David M. Rubenstein Rare Book, Manuscript and Special Collections Library's holdings on women and gender.
8. Sarah Dyer, "A Brief History of My Life in Zines," Duke University Libraries (website), http://library.duke.edu/digitalcollections/zines/dyer.html.
9. Ibid.
10. Dyer, online interview, November 2011.
11. Ibid.
12. *Sallie Bingham Center for Women's History and Culture* (website), http://library.duke.edu/rubenstein/ bingham/about.html.
13. Dyer, online interview, November 2011.
14. Kelly Wooten, interview, January 26, 2011.
15. Dyer, online interview, November 2011.

16. Ibid.

17. Ibid.

18. The Olympia Zine Library is located at Last Word Books in Olympia. When I visited the collection in May 2007, I discovered an impressive but disorderly collection housed in a closed-off room at the back of a used bookstore. Perhaps what was most remarkable about the collection is that I could not find anyone responsible for its maintenance. The young men running the bookstore explained that although they had "rescued" the collection from a volunteer collective, the collection had no designated custodian beyond visitors who occasionally chose to "tidy things up" (in fact, they even encouraged me to "tidy up," if I felt so inclined). When pressed to elaborate on the apparently self-sustaining nature of the collection, one of the owners compared it to Borges's "Library of Babel": "It's like Borges's library—infinite and unknowable. It has a life of its own—you never know what will disappear or show up" (Interview with Sky Cosby, Olympia, WA, May 2007). While the Olympia Zine Library is less orderly than many of the other community-based zine collections I visited over the course of my research, even larger and more formal collections, such as the Zine Library at ABC No Rio in New York and ZAPP housed at Richard Hugo House in Seattle, are structured by some of the same principles. In short, they are volunteer-run, and, as a result, even when "ordered," they are frequently structured by the idiosyncratic interests of individuals and collectives.

19. Dyer, online interview, November 2011.

20. Sarah Dyer Zine Collection (finding aid), http://library.duke.edu/rubenstein/findingaids/sarahdyercollection.

21. Wooten, interview, January 26, 2011.

22. For more information see "Major Zine Collections at the Bingham," http://library.duke.edu/ digitalcollections/zines.

23. Ibid.

24. For more information on the Sara Wood Zine Collection, see http://library.duke.edu/rubenstein/findingaids/woodsarah

25. Ibid.

26. Wooten, interview, January 26, 2011.

27. For a detailed discussion of this process, see Eichhorn, "D.I.Y. Collectors, Archiving Scholars, and Activist Librarians," 622–649.

28. Wooten, interview, January 26, 2011.

29. "The Mary Lily Research Grants," *Sallie Bingham Center for Women's History and Culture* (website), http://library.duke.edu/rubenstein/bingham/grants/index.html.

30. Kate Eichhorn, "Sites Unseen: Ethnographic Research in a Textual Community," *International Journal of Qualitative Studies in Education* 14 (2001): 565–578.

31. Among other publications, see Stephen Duncombe, *Notes from the Underground* (New York: Verso, 1997); Anna Poletti, *Intimate Ephemera:*

Reading Young Women's Lives in Australian Zine Culture (Melbourne: Melbourne University Press, 2008); and Adela Licona, *Zines in Third Space: Radical Cooperation and Borderlands Rhetoric* (Albany: State University of New York Press, 2012).

32. Alison Piepmeier, *Girl Zines: Making Media, Doing Feminism* (New York: New York University Press, 2009), 10.

33. Ibid.

34. Ibid., 29.

35. Wooten, interview, January 26, 2011.

36. *Sallie Bingham Center for Women's History and Culture* (website), http://library.duke.edu/rubenstein/ bingham/about.html.

37. Although there are, of course, exceptions, as one discovers in the archive, many second wave feminist presses were just as DIY as feminist zine producers in the 1990s and beyond. For example, in a press release for the 2nd Annual Lesbian Writers Conference, which took place in Chicago in September 1975, the organizers emphasize that "a special emphasis of this conference will be workshops and seminars on self-publishing and small press as practical alternatives for the Lesbian writer" (press release issued by WOMANPRESS, n.d., Atlanta Lesbian Feminist Association, Box 9, File 6, Sallie Bingham Center for Women's History and Culture, Duke University's David M. Rubenstein Rare Book & Manuscript Library). Self-publishing, much of it carried out on mimeograph machines, was arguably as important to the second wave feminist movement, or at least to the radical feminist movement, in the 1970s to 1980s as self-publishing proved to be to feminist activists and cultural producers in the 1990s.

38. Ibid.

39. Ibid.

40. Piepmeier, *Girl Zines*, 36.

41. Ibid., 29–30.

42. Ibid., 55.

43. Sara Marcus, "Zine Theory by Sara," *Out of the Vortex* 7 (1995): 3.

44. Ibid.

45. Sara Marcus, *Girls to the Front: The True Story of the Riot Grrrl Revolution* (New York: Harper Perennial, 2010), 6.

46. Marcus, "Zine Theory," 23.

47. Joan, *Out of the Vortex*, 7 (1995), 27.

48. *Hungry Girl Fanzine*, 2.

49. *Living Hell Lady*, 1.

50. *Function*, 5.

51. *Don't be a Pussy*.

52. *Femcore*.

53. Wooten, interview, January 26, 2011.

54. Piepmeier, *Girl Zines*, 4.

55. Hemmings, *Why Stories Matter*, 148.

56. Ibid.

57. Ibid.

58. Ibid., 150.

59. Ibid., 151.

60. Ibid.

61. Ibid., 13.

62. Janice Radway, "Zines, Half-Lives, and Afterlives: On the Temporalities of Social and Political Change," *PMLA* 126. 1 (2011): 148.

63. Cleo, *Slut Magnet*, 8 (1995).

64. Ibid.

65. Ibid.

66. Ibid.

3 / Archival Regeneration

1. Farai Chideya, Melissa Rossi, and Dogen Hannah, "Revolution, Girl Style," *Newsweek*, November 23, 1992, 84–86.

2. Marcus, *Girls to the Front*, 218.

3. For a discussion on Riot Grrrl's at least partial media blackout following the initial attention in 1992, see Marcus's *Girls to the Front*, 201–215.

4. Lisa Darms, interview, June 25, 2010.

5. Mark Asch, "NYU Libraries Acquire The Kathleen Hanna Papers for Their New 'Riot Grrrl Collection,'" *The L Magazine*, January 7, 2010, http://www.thelmagazine.com/TheMeasure/archives/2010/01/07/nyu-libraries-acquire-the-kathleen-hanna-papers-for-their-new-riot-grrrl-collection

6. As an example, one might consider the "semi-publics" or "intimate publics" fostered by Riot Grrrl zinesters who primarily distributed their publications at concerts, meetings, and by mail. This circulation strategy enabled them to develop a readership while continuing to control their audience. For an extended discussion, see Eichhorn, "Sites Unseen," 565–578, and Piepmeier, *Girl Zines*.

7. Darms, interview, June 25, 2010.

8. Among other postings, see "Read all about it: Riot Grrrl Collection" on the blog *The Girls Are* (http://thegirlsare.blogspot.com/2010/01/read-all-about-it-riot-grrrl-collection.html); "Feminist Sweepstakes" on *Jezebel* (http://jezebel.com/5443605/feminist-sweepstakes); "Kathleen Hanna Bequeaths Papers to NYU . . . " on *The Daily Swarm* (http://www.thedailyswarm.com/ headlines/kathleen-hanna-bequeaths-papers-nyu/); and "Kathleen Hanna Helps Make the Library Cool Again" on *Fader* (http://www.thefader.com/2010/11/17/interview-kathleen-hanna-on-the-raincoats-and-building-an-archive/).

9. Pierre Bourdieu, *The Field of Cultural Production*, ed. Randal Johnson (New York: Columbia University Press, 1993) 30–31.

10. Ibid.

11. Ibid.

12. Ibid.

13. Ibid., 49.

14. Michel Foucault, "Of Other Spaces," *Diacritics* 16 (Spring 1986): 22–27.

15. Details about the Fales Library and Special Collections and finding aids for specific collections are available on their website at http://www.nyu. edu/library/bobst/research/fales

16. Mike Lindgren, January 7, 2010 (4:09 p.m.), comment on Mark Asch, "NYU Libraries Acquire The Kathleen Hanna Papers for Their New 'Riot Grrrl Collection,'" *The L Magazine*, January 7, 2010.

17. Mike Cocklin, January 7, 2010 (10:03 p.m.), comment on Mark Asch, "NYU Libraries Acquire The Kathleen Hanna Papers for Their New 'Riot Grrrl Collection,'" *The L Magazine*, January 7, 2010.

18. Emily, "Kathleen Hanna & Riot Grrrl Archives at NYU," *Jukebox Heroines* (blog), January 28, 2010, http://jukeboxheroines.wordpress. com/2010/01/28/kathleen-hanna-riot-grrrl-archives-at-nyu

19. Erin Fairchild, January 8, 2010 (1:18 p.m.), comment on Mark Asch, "NYU Libraries Acquire The Kathleen Hanna Papers for Their New 'Riot Grrrl Collection,'" *The L Magazine*, January 7, 2010.

20. Mary Halford, "Quiet Riot," *The New Yorker*, January 12, 2010, accessed on January 8, 2011, http://www.newyorker.com/online/blogs/ books/2010/01/quiet-riot.html

21. Alyx Vesey, "Kathleen Hanna, Archival Subject," *Feminist Music Geek* (blog), January 8, 2010, http://feministmusicgeek.com/2010/01/08/ kathleen-hanna-archival-subject

22. As Lisa Darms explained, "a lot of the challenges or unusual things about the Riot Grrrl Collection, I've already dealt with in the Downtown, like the fact that I have living donors" (interview, June 25, 2010).

23. Kathleen Hanna was born in 1968, and the vast majority of the women whose papers are housed in the collection were born in the early 1970s. Moreover, while some women represented in the collection are no longer active as musicians, most of the donors continue to engage in some form of cultural production. Becca Albee, for example, was a member of Excuse 17 in the early to mid 1990s; she is now a New York City-based visual artist and professor of art.

24. Cvetkovich, *Archive of Feelings*, 242.

25. Darms, interview, June 25, 2010.

26. Ibid.

27. Ibid.

28. Ibid.

29. Ibid.

30. Ibid.

31. Ibid.

32. Ibid.

33. Johanna Fateman, online interview, August 2010.

34. Kathleen Hanna, online interview, August 2010.

35. Ibid.

36. Ibid.

37. It is important to bear in mind the fact that collecting the papers of individuals does not necessarily mean that the research carried out in the collection will focus on individuals rather than the movement as a whole. Indeed, when Lisa Darms read a draft of this chapter, she emphasized that, to date, researchers visiting the Riot Grrrl Collection have come to carry out research not on individual Riot Grrrls, such as Kathleen Hanna, but rather on broader subjects related to feminism, art, music, and performance. On this basis, she strongly advised against concluding that the structure of the collection will necessarily dictate how the collection is ultimately used by researchers.

38. In this respect, it is by no means insignificant that Riot Grrrl NYC, which appeared after groups were established Olympia and D.C., was unique in both its demographic (Riot Grrrl NYC attracted younger women as well as women well into their thirties) and its emphasis on creative work. If other Riot Grrrl groups were primarily activist-oriented, the New York movement was more focused on art. As Marcus notes, "In addition to making zines, the chapter organized exhibitions of members' artwork and put on rock shows at local venues" (*Girls to the Front*, 291). On this basis, the location of the Riot Grrrl papers at Fales Library is arguably consistent with the form Riot Grrrl took in New York from its inception.

39. For more information on the ACT UP Oral History Project, go to: http://www.actuporalhistory.org/

40. Kathleen Hanna, "When the Worlds that once Liberated You Become Bars on yr Cage—random notes on political depression" (unpublished essay), Riot Grrrl Collection (Johanna Fateman, Series III. Box I, Folder 64), Fales Library and Special Collections.

41. Marcus, *Girls to the Front*, 241.

42. Marvin Taylor, discussion, February 25, 2011.

43. Darms, interview, June 25, 2010.

44. Ibid.

45. See, for example, Dick Hebdige, *Subculture: The Meaning of Style* (London: Routledge, 1979), and Tricia Rose, *Black Noise: Rap Music and Black Culture in Contemporary America* (Hanover, CT: Wesleyan University Press, 1994).

46. Darms, interview, June 25, 2010.

47. Cvetkovich, *Archive of Feelings*, 245.

48. Ibid., 245.

49. Ibid.

50. Indy Grrrl and The Girls Are, January 12, 2010 (2:25 and 10:26 p.m.), comments on "Read All About It: Riot Grrrl Collection," *The Girls Are* (blog), January 11, 2010, http://thegirlsare.blogspot.com/2010/01/read-all-about-it-riot-grrrl-collection.html

51. "The Fales Library at NYU's Riot Grrl Collection," *The Village Voice*, November 3, 2010, http://www.villagevoice.com/bestof/2010/award/best-way-to-disseminate-feminist-punk-culture-through-a-public-institution-2167594/

52. Fran, November 3, 2010 (9:28 p.m.), comment on "The Fales Library at NYU's Riot Grrl Collection," *The Village Voice*, November 3, 2010.

53. Darms, interview, June 25, 2010.

54. Ibid.

55. Ibid.

56. Hanna, online interview, August 2010.

57. Fateman, online interview, August 2010.

58. Hanna, online interview, August 2010.

59. For a detailed discussion on the semipublic nature of girl zine networks, see Kate Eichhorn, "Sites Unseen," 565–578.

60. Darms, interview, June 25, 2010.

61. Ibid.

62. Hanna, online interview, August 2010.

63. For example, Riot Grrrl Collection donor, Becca Albee (a visual artist and former member of the band Excuse 17) attended Evergreen State College in the early 1990s. While there, she enrolled in a course on women's health. According to Albee, as part of the course, students were required to purchase a speculum and perform self-examinations on several occasions throughout the semester; the self-examinations notably took place *in* the classroom on class time. Albee's personal recollection offers insight into Evergreen's pedagogy and politics when Riot Grrrl was taking shape in Olympia in the early 1990s (Becca Albee, discussion, January 2010).

64. Kathleen Eichhorn, "Cyborg Grrrls: New Technologies, Identities and Community in the Production of 'Zines" (master's thesis, Simon Fraser University, 1996), 156n78.

65. Darms, interview, June 25, 2010.

66. After writing this paragraph, I realized I had repeatedly used the word "moment" in reference to the theoretical and political climate under which Riot Grrrl took shape in the early 1990s. Upon reflection, I stand by my word choice. Coming after the establishment of Women's Studies departments and at the height of feminist and queer theory and just before the widespread decline of second wave feminist institutions, 1989 to 1993 represented a brief reprieve from more pressing battles. After all, at least for those us who were privileged enough to spend these years cloistered away on university campuses, it was a time when one could realistically imagine turning attention to more esoteric concerns without risking the immediate loss of any previous political gains. As discussed in previous chapters of this book, the subsequent collapse of second wave feminist institutions proved this to be a naïve assumption.

67. Miscellaneous photocopied articles, Kathleen Hanna Collection (unprocessed at the time of access), Riot Grrrl Collection, Fales Library and Special Collections, NYU, New York, NY.

68. Joanne Gottlieb and Gayle Wald, "Smells Like Teen Spirit: Riot Grrrl, Revolution and Women in Independent Rock" in *Microphone Fiends: Youth Music & Youth Culture*, eds. Andrew Ross and Tricia Rose (New York: Routledge, 1994), 263

69. Gayle Wald, "Just a Girl?: Rock Music, Feminism, and the Cultural Construction of Female Youth." *Signs: Journal of Women in Culture and Society* 23.3 (Spring 1998): 588.

70. Ibid., 593.

71. Fateman, online interview, August 2010.

72. Ibid.

73. Ibid.

74. Marion Leonard, *Gender in the Music Industry* (Burlington: Ashgate Publishing Company, 2007), 115.

75. Ibid., 124.

76. Ibid.

77. Darms, interview, June 25, 2010.

78. Bourdieu, *Field of Cultural Production*, 59.

79. Fateman, online interview, August 2010.

80. Johanna Fateman, Kathleen Hanna, and Jocelyn Samson, "Hot Topic," *Le Tigre* (San Francisco: Mr. Lady Records, 1998).

81. C. Carr, "Theoretical Girl: The Legacy of Kathy Acker," *The Village Voice*, November 5, 2002, 49.

82. Ibid.

83. Marcus, *Girls to the Front*, 32.

84. Although I know this quotation is taken directly from a Riot Grrrl zine published in the early 1990s, I no longer know the source. In my thesis on Riot Grrrl zines, rather than cite the author or zine, I simply included a note that reads, "I have decided that it would be best to not indicate the name of the writer or 'zine.'" The fact that I felt ethically obligated to protect the identity of the zine producer may now strike the reader as strange, but at the time I had a strong sense that I was researching a community and its semipublic papers and was thereby obligated to protect the identities of my "participants" in the same way an ethnographer might conceal or change the names of research subjects. While such consideration may no longer be relevant, my early decision as a researcher raises important questions about the migration of Riot Grrrl materials into the archive. If there was such a strong sense of the semipublic status of zines in the early to mid 1990s when they were first put into circulation, what is their status in the archive now? Do we treat them as publications or personal papers? While the archivists and librarians I interviewed for this study reported little if any contact with former zine producers objecting to their zines being placed in publically

accessible collections without their permission, I maintain that the ambiguity of the documents at their time of production is something that may, in some cases, still need to be taken into account.

85. See note 84 for explanation.
86. See, for example, Hebdige's discussion of bricolage in *Subculture*.
87. Godard, "Feminist Periodicals and the Production of Cultural Value," 211.
88. Ibid.
89. Ibid.

4 / Radical Catalogers and Accidental Archivists

1. Lily Koppel, "Zines in the Library Catalog, Of Course," *New York Times*, April 11, 2006, http://www.nytimes.com/2006/04/11/nyregion/11ink.html.
2. *Radical Reference*, accessed on March 9, 2012, http://radicalreference.info.
3. Colin Moynihan, "For $1, a Collective Mixing Art and Radical Politics Turns Itself Into Its Own Landlord," *New York Times*, July 4, 2006, http://www.nytimes.com /2006/07/04/nyregion/04abc.html?_r=1.
4. ABC No Rio Zine Library, access on March 9, 2012, http://www.abcnorio.org/ facilities/zine_library.html.
5. Moynihan, "For $1."
6. *Lower East Side Librarian*, http://lowereastsidelibrarian.info.
7. "Life on Campus: A Living and Learning Community," Barnard College website, access on March 20, 2012, http://barnard.edu/admissions/campus/life-on-campus.
8. Neil Smith reports that following the Tompkins Square riots in 1990, which erupted after the police attempted to forcibly remove homeless residents from the park, the City spent an estimated $14 million dollars redesigning the park ($4 million on infrastructural "improvements," which included benches with wrought iron dividers to prohibit sleeping and enforced gates, and $10 million on policing). See Neil Smith, "After Tompkins Square Park: Degentrification and the Revanchist City," *Re-presenting the City: Ethnicity, Capital, and Culture in the 21th-Century Metropolis*, ed. Anthony D. King (New York: New York University Press, 1996), 100.
9. Freedman, interview, April 17, 2012.
10. Jenna Freedman, "The Zines are in Charge: A Radical Reference Librarian in the Archives," *Metropolitan Archivist* 18.1 (2012): 18, 19.
11. Ibid.
12. Ibid.
13. Jenna Freedman, "Your Zine Toolkit, A DIY Collection," *Library Journal*, June 15, 2006, http://www.libraryjournal.com/article/CA6341863.html.
14. Jenna Freedman, "Collection Proposal: Women's Studies Zines at Barnard College—Pilot Project" (June 2003), http://zines.barnard.edu/proposal.

15. Freedman, interview, April 17, 2012.

16. Ibid.

17. For more information, see "About the Collection" on the Barnard Zine Library website at http://zines.barnard.edu/about-barnard-zines/aboutthecollection.

18. For more information, see "What is WorldCat?" on the WorldCat website at http://www.worldcat.org/whatis/default.jsp.

19. Freedman, interview, April 17, 2012.

20. Jenna Freedman, "AACR 2—Bendable but Not Flexible: Cataloging Zines at Barnard College," in *Radical Cataloging: Essays at the Front*, ed. K. R. Roberto (Jefferson, NC: McFarland & Company, Inc., 2008), 233.

21. Ibid.

22. Jenna Freedman, "Grrrl Zines in the Library," *Signs: Journal of Women in Culture and Society* 35.1 (2009): 58–59.

23. Freedman, interview, April 17, 2012.

24. Ibid.

25. Freedman, "The Zines are in Charge," 19.

26. Ibid.

27. Ibid.

28. Ibid., 18.

29. For more information on Critical Mass, see Chris Carlsson, ed. *Critical Mass: Bicycling's Defiant Celebration* (San Francisco: AK Press, 2002).

30. Emily Drabinski, "Gendered S(h)elves: Body and identity in the Library," *Women & Environments International Magazine* 78/79 (Fall 2009/Winter 2010): 17.

31. "Library of Congress Classifications," Library of Congress website, accessed on May 1, 2012, http://www.loc.gov/catdir/cpso/lcc.html.

32. Ibid.

33. As cited in Jane A. Rosenberg, "Foundation for Service: The 1896 Hearings on the Library of Congress," *The Journal of Library of History* 21.1 (Winter 1986): 117.

34. Ibid.

35. Sanford Berman, *Prejudices and Antipathies: A Tract on the LC Subject Heads Concerning People* (Metuchen, NJ: Scarecrow Press, 1971), ix.

36. Ibid., ix-x.

37. Ibid., x.

38. Ibid., 178.

39. Ibid.

40. Ibid., 182.

41. Ibid., 215.

42. Ibid.

43. Patricia Glass Schuman and Kathleen Weibel, "The Woman Arisen," *American Libraries* (June 1979), 322–323.

44. Ibid., 325.

45. Joan Marshall, *On Equal Terms: A Thesaurus for Nonsexist Indexing and Cataloging* (New York: Neal-Schuman, 1977), 4.

46. Ibid., 7.

47. Ibid.

48. Ibid.

49. Bradley Dilger and William Thompson, "Ubiquitous Cataloging," in *Radical Cataloging: Essays at the Front*, ed. K. R. Roberto (Jefferson, NC: McFarland & Company, Inc., 2008), 40.

50. Drabinski, "Gendered S(h)elves," 17.

51. Ibid.

52. Ibid.

53. Ibid.

54. tatiana de la tierra, "Latina Lesbian subject Headings: The Power of Naming," in *Radical Cataloging: Essays at the Front*, 98.

55. Freedman, interview, April 17, 2012.

56. I had known Jenna Freedman for several years before I came to truly appreciate and understand her activist work at the level of the library catalog. As a researcher who, prior to writing this book, understood very little about the construction of library catalogs or the labor of cataloging, I initially had difficulty even understanding what I perceived as Freedman's cataloging preoccupation. Over the course of working on this book and collaborating with Freedman on several public panels, I have gained an appreciation for how her work as a collector and cataloger impacts my own work as a researcher and educator. I have also become aware of the fact that the invisibility of the scholarly work carried out by librarians perpetuates hierarchies within our own workplaces. Working on this book and coming to understand the extent to which the often invisible labor of librarians and archivists shapes my own research and teaching, I now recognize the extent to which they are always already our collaborators and even coauthors, and I wish to impress upon my readers precisely such concerns throughout this chapter.

57. Geraldine Ostrove (Senior Policy Specialist, Policy and Standards Division, Library of Congress), email message to author, June 5, 2012.

58. Results reflect a search carried out on June 1, 2012; because new materials are always being added to the catalog, however, results carried out after this date will invariably be different.

59. WorldCat (accessed May 15, 2012), http://www.worldcat.org.

60. CLIO (accessed May 15, 2012), http://clio.cul.columbia.edu:7018/vwebv/ search?search Code1=GKEY&searchType=2&argType1=any&searchArg1=OCM61886390

61. Freedman, interview, April 17, 2012.

62. Jenna Freedman, "Dear Library of Congress, please add cross references to—WAVE FEMINISMS," Lower East Side Librarian (blog), April 22, 2008, http://lowereastsidelibrarian.info/feminismcrossreferences.

63. Ibid.

64. See Hemmings, *Why Stories Matter.*

65. CLIO (accessed May 15, 2012), http://clio.cul.columbia.edu:7018/vwebv/holdingsInfo?searchId=3783&recCount=25&recPointer=0&bibId=4791411

66. Freedman, "The Zines are in Charge," 19.

67. Ibid., 238.

68. Drabinski, "Gendered S(h)elves," 18.

69. Michel Foucault, *The Order of Things* (New York: Vintage Books, 1994), xv.

70. Ibid.

71. Ibid.

72. Ibid., xx.

73. Donna Haraway, *Simians, Cyborgs, and Women: The Reinvention of Nature* (New York: Routledge, 1991), 175.

74. Ibid.

75. Lorraine Code, *Rhetorical Spaces: Essays on Gendered Locations* (New York: Routledge, 1995), 29.

Conclusion

1. Cvetkovich, *Archive of Feelings*, 245.

2. Ibid., 246.

3. For more information see the Queer Zine Archive Project (QZAP) at http://www.qzap.org/v6/index.php.

4. Freedman, interview, April 17, 2012.

5. Darms, interview, June 25, 2012.

6. Michelle Dean, "The Struggle for the Occupy Wall Street Archives," *The AWL* (December 21, 2011), http://www.theawl.com/2011/12/the-struggle-for-the-occupy-wall-street-archives.

7. Marcus, *Girls to the Front*, 8–9.

Works Cited

Archiving Women Conference. http://www.socialdifference.org/events/
archiving-women-0

Asch, Mark. "NYU Libraries Acquire The Kathleen Hanna Papers for
Their New 'Riot Grrrl Collection.'" *The L Magazine*, January 7, 2010,
http://www.thelmagazine.com/TheMeasure/archives/2010/01/07/
nyu-libraries-acquire-the-kathleen-hanna-papers-for-their-
new-riot-grrrl-collection

Berlant, Lauren. "'68, or Something." *Critical Inquiry* 21.1 (Autumn
1994): 124–155.

Berman, Sanford. *Prejudices and Antipathies: A Tract on the LC Subject Heads Concerning People*. Metuchen, NJ: Scarecrow Press, Inc.,
1971.

Bly, Liz, and Kelly Wooten, eds. *Make Your Own History: Documenting Feminist and Queer Activism in the 21st Century*. Sacramento:
Litwin Books, 2012.

Bourdieu, Pierre. *The Field of Cultural Production*. New York: Columbia University Press, 1993.

Brown, Wendy. *Politics Out of History*. Princeton: Princeton University Press, 2001.

Burton, Antoinette. "Introduction." *Archive Stories: Facts Fictions,
and the Writing of History*. Durham: Duke University Press, 2005.

Carr, C. "Theoretical Girl: The Legacy of Kathy Acker." *The Village
Voice* (November 5, 2002), 49.

Carlsson, Chris. Ed. *Critical Mass: Bicycling's Defiant Celebration*. San Francisco: AK Press, 2002.

Chideya, Farai, Melissa Rossi and Dogen Hannah. "Revolution, Girl Style." *Newsweek* (November 23, 1992), 84–86.

Cleo, *Slut Magnet*, 8 (1995).

Cvetkovich, Ann. *An Archive of Feelings*. Durham: Duke University Press, 2003.

Chester, Gail. "The Anthology as a Medium for Feminist Debate." *Women's Studies International Forum* 25.2 (2002): 193–207.

Code, Lorraine. *Rhetorical Spaces: Essays on Gendered Locations*. New York: Routledge, 1995.

Derrida, Jacques. *Archive Fever: A Freudian Impression*. Translated by Eric Prenowitz. Chicago: University of Chicago Press, 1996.

Dean, Michelle. "The Struggle for the Occupy Wall Street Archives," The AWL (December 21, 2011), http://www.theawl.com/2011/12/the-struggle-for-the-occupy-wall-street-archives.

Dilger, Bradley, and William Thompson. "Ubiquitous Cataloging." In Radical Cataloging: Essays at the Front, edited by K. R. Roberto. 40-52. Jefferson, NC: McFarland & Company, Inc., 2008.

Dinshaw, Carolyn. *Getting Medieval: Sexualities and Communities, Pre- and Postmodern*. Durham: Duke University Press, 1999.

Drabinski, Emily. "Gendered S(h)elves: Body and identity in the Library." *Women & Environments International Magazine* 78/79 (Fall 2009/Winter 2010): 16–18, 43.

Duncombe, Stephen. *Notes from the Underground*. New York: Verso, 1997.

Dyer, Sarah. "A Brief History of My Life in Zines." *Duke University Libraries* (website), http://library.duke.edu/digitalcollections/zines/dyer.html.

Eichhorn, Kate. "D.I.Y. Collectors, Archiving Scholars and Activist Librarians." *Women's Studies: An Interdisciplinary Journal* 39 (2010): 622–646.

———. "Archival Genres: Gathering Texts and Reading Spaces." *Invisible Culture* 12 (Spring 2008). http://www.rochester.edu/ in_visible_culture/Issue_12/eichhorn/index.htm.

Eichhorn, Kathleen. "Cyborg Grrrls: New Technologies, Identities and Community in the Production of 'Zines." Master's thesis, Simon Fraser University, 1996.

Ernst, Wolfgang. "Archival Action: The Archive as ROM and Its Political Instrumentalization under National Socialism." *History of Human Sciences* 12.2 (1999): 13–34.

Fales Library and Special Collections. http://www.nyu.edu/ library/ bobst/research/fales>

"The Fales Library at NYU's Riot Grrl Collection." *The Village Voice* (November 3, 2010), http://www.villagevoice.com/bestof/2010/ award/best-way-to-disseminate-feminist-punk-culture-through-a-public-institution-2167594/

Faludi, Susan. "American Electra: Feminism's Ritual Matricide." *Harper's Magazine* (October 2010), 29–41.

Firestone, Shulamith, and Anne Koedt, eds. *Notes from the Second Year: Women's Liberation: Major Writings of the Radical Feminists* (New York, 1970).

Foucault, Michel. *The Archaeology of Knowledge*. New York: Pantheon Books, 1972.

———. *Language, Counter-Memory, Practice: Selected Essays and Interviews*. Edited by Donald F. Bouchard. Translated by Donald F. Bouchard and Sherry Simon. Ithaca: Cornell University Press, 1977.

———. "Of Other Spaces." *Diacritics* 16 (Spring 1986): 22–27.

———. *The Order of Things*. New York: Vintage Books, 1994.

Freeman, Elizabeth. *Time Binds: Queer Temporalities, Queer Histories*. Durham: Duke University Press, 2010.

Freedman, Jenna. "AACR 2—Bendable but Not Flexible: Cataloging Zines at Barnard College." *Radical Cataloging: Essays at the Front* edited by K.R. Roberto, 231--240. NC: McFarland & Company, Inc., 2008.s Studies Zines at Barnard College—Pilot Project" (June 2003), http://zines.barnard.edu/proposal.

———. "Grrrl Zines in the Library." *Signs: Journal of Women in Culture and Society*, 35, 1 (2009): 52–59.

———. "Archiving Women Report Back," *Lower East Side Librarian* (blog), February 2, 2009, http://lowereastsidelibrarian.info/report-back/ archivingwomen

———. "Your Zine Toolkit, A DIY Collection." *Library Journal*, June 15, 2006, http://www.libraryjournal.com/article/CA6341863.html.

———. "The Zines are in Charge: A Radical Reference Librarian in the Archives." *Metropolitan Archivist*, 19 (Winter 2012): 18–19 & 41.

Fritzsche, Peter. "The Archive." *History & Memory* 17.1/2 (2005): 13–44.

Giroux, Henry. "Terror of Neoliberalism: Rethinking the Significance of Cultural Politics." *College Literature* 32.1 (Winter 2005): 1–19.

Godard, Barbara. "Feminist Periodicals and the Production of Cultural Value: The Canadian Context." *Women's Studies International Forum* 25.2 (2002): 209–223.

Gottlieb, Joanne, and Gayle Wald. "Smells Like Teen Spirit: Riot Grrrl, Revolution and Women in Independent Rock." *Microphone Fiends: Youth Music & Youth Culture.* Edited by Andrew Ross and Tricia Rose, 250–274. New York: Routledge, 1994.

de Haan, Francisca. "Getting to the Source: A 'Truly International' Archive for the Women's Movement (IAV, now IIAV): From its Foundation in Amsterdam in 1935 to the Return of its Looted Archives in 2003." *Journal of Women's History* 16.4 (Winter 2004): 148–172.

Halberstam, Judith. *Female Masculinity.* Durham: Duke University Press, 1998.

———. *In a Queer Time & Place.* Durham: Duke University Press, 2005.

Halford, Mary. "Quiet Riot." *The New Yorker,* January 12, 2010, http://www.newyorker.com/online/blogs/books/2010/01/quiet-riot.html

Haraway, Donna. *Simians, Cyborgs, and Women: The Reinvention of Nature.* New York: Routledge, 1991.

Harvey, David. "Neoliberalism as Creative Destruction." *Annals of the American Academy of Political and Social Science* 610 (March 2007): 21–44.

———. *Spaces of Neoliberalism: Towards a Theory of Uneven Geographical Development.* Stuttgart: Steiner, 2005.

Hebdige, Dick. *Subculture: The Meaning of Style.* London: Routledge, 1979.

Hemmings, Clare. *Why Stories Matter: The Political Grammar of Feminist Theory.* Durham: Duke University Press, 2010.

Henry, Astrid. "Enviously Grateful, Gratefully Envious: The Dynamics of Generational Relationships in U.S. Feminism." *Women's Studies Quarterly* 34.3/4 (2006): 140–153.

Hildenbrand, Suzanne, ed. *Women's Collections: Libraries, Archives, and Consciousness.* New York: The Haworth Press, 1986.

Joreen, "The Bitch Manifesto." *Notes from the Second Year: Writings of the Radical Feminists.* Edited by Shulamith Firestone and Anne Koedt. (1970).

Kimbell Relph, Anne. "The World Center for Women's Archives, 1935–1940." *Signs* 4.3 (1979): 597–603.

Koppel, Lily. "Zines in the Library Catalog, Of Course," *New York Times,* April 11, 2006, http://www.nytimes.com/2006/04/11/nyregion/11ink.html.

Kumbier, Alana. *Ephemeral Material: Queering Archives.* Sacramento: Litwin Books, 2013.

Leonard, Marion. *Gender in the Music Industry*. Burlington: Ashgate Publishing Company, 2007.

Licona, Adela. *Zines in Third Space: Radical Cooperation and Border-lands Rhetoric*. Albany: State University of New York Press, 2012.

Lower East Side Librarian, http://lowereastsidelibrarian.info.

Marcus, Sara. *Girls to the Front: The True Story of the Riot Grrrl Revolution*. New York: Harper Perennial, 2010.

Marshall, Joan. *On Equal Terms: A Thesaurus for Nonsexist Indexing and Cataloging*. New York: Neal-Schuman, 1977.

Manoff, Marlene. "Theories of the Archive from Across the Disciplines." *Libraries and the Academy* 4.1 (2004): 9–25.

Moynihan, Colin. "For $1, a Collective Mixing Art and Radical Politics Turns Itself Into Its Own Landlord." *New York Times*, July 4, 2006, http://www.nytimes.com /2006/07/04/nyregion/04abc.html?_r=1.

———. "Homesteading a Little Place in History; Archive Documents Squatters' Movement on Lower East Side." *New York Times*, December 8, 2003. http://www.nytimes.com/2003/12/08/nyregion/homesteading-little-place-history-archive-documents-squatters-movementlower.html?page wanted=all&src=pm.

Murray, Simone. *Mixed Media: Feminist Presses and Publishing Politics*. London: Pluto Press, 2004.

Out of the Vortex, 7 (1995).

Piepmeier, Alison. *Girl Zines: Making Media, Doing Feminism*. New York: New York University Press, 2009.

Poletti, Anna. *Intimate Ephemera: Reading Young Women's Lives in Australian Zine Culture*. Melbourne: Melbourne University Press, 2008.

Radway, Janice. *Reading the Romance: Women, Patriarchy, and Popular Literature*. Chapel Hill: University of North Carolina Press, 1984.

———. "Zines, Half-Lives, and Afterlives: On the Temporalities of Social and Political Change." *PMLA* 126.1 (2011): 140–150.

Ridener, John. *From Polders to Postmodernism: A Concise History of Archival Theory*. Duluth: Litwin Books, LLC, 2009.

Riot Grrrlz Outer Space. *The Bitch Manifesto* (zine) (n.d.).

Roberto, K. R., ed. *Radical Cataloging: Essays at the Front*. Jefferson, NC: McFarland & Company, Inc., 2008.

Rose, Tricia. *Black Noise: Rap Music and Black Culture in Contemporary America*. Hanover, CT: Wesleyan University Press, 1994).

Rosenberg, Jane A. "Foundation for Service: The 1896 Hearings on the Library of Congress." *The Journal of Library of History* 21.1 (Winter 1986): 107–130.

Schuman, Patricia Glass, and Kathleen Weibel. "The Woman Arisen." *American Libraries* (June 1979), 322–324.

Smith, Neil. "After Tomkins Square Park: Degentrification and the Revanchist City." *Re-presenting the City: Ethnicity, Capital, and Culture in the 21th-Century Metropolis.* Edited by Anthony D. King. New York: New York University Press, 1996.

Steedman, Carolyn. *Dust: The Archive and Cultural History.* New Brunswick: Rutgers University Press, 2002.

Stoler, Ann Laura. *Along the Archival Grain: Epistemic Anxieties and Colonial Common Sense.* Princeton: Princeton University Press, 2009.

Taylor, Diana. *The Archive and the Repertoire: Performing Cultural Memory in the Americas.* Durham: Duke University Press, 2003.

de la tierra, Tatiana. "Latina Lesbian subject Headings: The Power of Naming." In *Radical Cataloging: Essays at the Front,* edited by K. R. Roberto. 94-102. Jefferson, NC: McFarland & Company, Inc., 2008.

Travis, Trysh. "The Women in Print Movement: History and Implications." *Book History* 11 (2008): 275–300.

Voss-Hubbard, Anke. "'No Document—No History': Mary Ritter Beard and the Early History of Women's Archives." *The American Archivist* 58.1 (Winter 1995): 16–30.

Wald, Gayle. "Just a Girl?: Rock Music, Feminism, and the Cultural Construction of Female Youth." *Signs: Journal of Women in Culture and Society* 23.3 (Spring 1998): 585–610.

World Center for Women's Archives, Inc. *Brief report of World Center for Women's Archives* (Pamphlet) (November 13, 1939).

INDEX

ABC No Rio, 125, 168n18
ACT UP, 10, 99, 101; activism, 100–101; archives, 10; Oral History Project, 10, 99
Action Girl Comics, 57
Action Girl Newsletter, 64
Affect, viii, 3, 82, 88, 92, 94, 96
Albee, Becca, 86, 171n23, 173n63
Aletta, Institute for Women's History, 41, 166n30. *See also* International Archives for the Women's Movement
American Library Association (ALA), 132, 135, 138; bulletin, 136; task force on sexism in subject headings, 138
Amy Mariaskin Zine Collection, 66
Archival proximity, 60–61
Archives: digital, 5, 23, 153, 156, 162n10; feminist, 3, 9, 19, 30–32, 41, 43–44, 49, 53–55, 56, 78, 155–156; queer, x, 30; university, ix, 15, 32, 65–66, 157; women's, 1–3, 32–50, 98, 157
Archiving Women (conference), 1–2, 161n1

Avant garde, 22, 88–92, 110–112, 114–119; feminist, 114–121; movements, 88–92

Barnard College, 123–125. *See also* Barnard Zine Library
Barnard Zine Library, 1, 4, 22, 98, 123–153, 162n10
Beard, Mary, 33, 34, 35, 39
Berlant, Lauren, 51–53
Berman, Sanford, 136–138, 142, 148
Bikini Kill, vii, 88, 93, 95
Bitch Manifesto, 57–61, 79
Bourdieu, Pierre, 22, 88, 90, 114, 119, 120, 170
Bricolage, 118
Brown, Wendy, 7–9, 17
Butler, Judy, 109

Cataloging, 1, 22, 23, 123–153
Code, Lorraine, 152
Copy machine, vii, ix, 71, 92, 107, 108
Critical Mass, 133–134, 142–143
Cultural Studies, 18, 20
Cvetkovich, Ann, xii, 5, 18, 19, 30, 94, 102, 109, 155–156

Darms, Lisa, xii, 22, 85, 86, 87, 95–98, 101–107, 113, 114, 118, 156, 171n22, 172n37

Derrida, Jacques, 4, 5, 7, 108–109

Dinshaw, Carolyn, 30

DIY, 10, 29, 32, 86, 98, 104, 120, 127, 132, 156–157, 162n10

Downtown Collection, 90, 96, 101, 102, 113

Drabinski, Emily, xii, 2, 134, 141

Duke University, 2, 4, 14, 15, 21, 55–84, 91, 94, 98

Dunye, Cheryl, 19

Dyer, Sarah, 15, 21, 56, 57, 59, 61–67

Edel, Deborah, 47

Evergreen State College, 87, 95, 99, 106–107, 110, 173n63

E-zines, 128

Fales Library and Special Collections, 4, 22, 85–121

Faludi, Susan, xiii, 21, 25–26, 28, 31, 77

Fateman, Johanna, 22, 97, 100, 104–105, 111, 112, 114

Feminism: activism, vii, viii, ix, 3, 6, 15, 20, 26–27, 31, 33–34, 37, 39, 41, 42, 46, 63, 65, 77, 100, 143, 146, 148, 158, 162n10; art, 27–29, 90, 93, 95, 110, 114–115, 118, 119; first wave feminism, 20, 32–44, 72, 146–148, 158; intergenerational conflict, viii-ix, 21, 25–29, 31, 53, 56, 61, 77–79; librarianship, 134, 138, 140; literature, 108–119; music, 27, 66, 93, 94, 110, 111, 112, 120, 143, 171n23 (see also Riot Grrrl); radical feminism, 12, 16, 27, 48, 58, 69, 111, 146, 163–164n33, 169n37; second wave feminism viii, ix, 3–4, 8, 11–14, 22, 42–50, 54, 59, 67, 70, 71, 72, 74, 76, 80, 107, 109, 116, 146–148, 158, 164n41, 169n37, 173n66; theory, 72, 76–80, 140–141; third wave feminism, viii, 21, 63–65, 67–72, 129–130, 133, 143, 146, 148–149, 162n10, 164n41

Firestone, Shulamith, 59

Foucault, Michel, 4, 7, 15, 90, 151

Freedman, Jenna, xii, 1, 2, 20, 22, 98, 106, 123–133, 138, 141–153, 156, 177n56

Freeman, Elizabeth, 9, 20, 25, 27–29, 53

Freeman, Joreen, 58–61

Gender-queer, 98, 126

Gender Studies xi, 25–26, 132, 146. *See also* Women's Studies

Genealogical Politics, 7, 9, 20, 31

Genealogy, 7–9

Girl Zines: Making Media, Doing Feminism, x, 67–69, 71, 118

Girls Empowering Resisting Labels and Limits (GERLL), 66

Girls to the Front: The True Story of the Riot Grrrl Revolution, 72, 74, 85, 100, 116, 159, 172n38

Godard, Barbara, xi, 10, 120–121

Grier, Barbara, 11

Halberstam, Judith, 17, 19, 29, 30

Hanna, Kathleen, 22, 86–87, 91–93, 95, 97–98, 100, 103–117, 171n23

Haraway, Donna, 152

Harvey, David, 5

Hemmings, Clare, 21, 55, 76–80, 149

Henry, Astrid, 3

Henry, Liz, 57, 167n6

Hildenbrand, Suzanne, 32, 44–45

I'm so Fucking Beautiful, 75

International Archives for the Women's Movement (IAV), 32, 37, 38, 40–43

Jacobs, Aletta, 37

Koedt, Anne, 59

L Magazine, 86–87, 91–93

Le Tigre, 95, 114

Lesbian, 16, 28, 47–49, 76, 78, 81, 100–102, 108, 109, 110, 137, 138, 141–142, 149–150, 155–156, 169n37

Lesbian Herstory Archives (LHA), 18, 45, 47–50, 156

Library of Congress: classification system, 135, 141–142; subject headings, 136–139, 143–146, 148–149
Lower East Side Librarian (blog), 2, 125, 146
Lower East Side Librarian Winter Solstice Shout Out, 124, 146
Lower East Side Squatter and Homesteaders Archives, 10

Manus, Rosa, 37, 40, 54
Marcus, Sara, 72–76, 85, 100–101, 116, 159, 172n38
Marshall, Joan, 139–142
Mimeograph, 69, 71, 169n37
Morgan, Robin, viii
Murray, Simone, 11, 13
Myles, Eileen, 113, 115

National Women's Liberation Front for Librarians (NWLFFL), 139
Neoliberalism, 5–11, 47, 146
The Nerdy Grrrl Revolution, 75
Nestle, Joan, 47
Newsweek, 74, 85–86, 88, 114
Notes from the Second Year, 58–59, 61

Occupy Movement: library; 158 archive, 158–159
off our backs, 74–76
Olympia, WA, 65, 85, 87, 95–102, 113
Olympia Zine Library, 65, 168n18
On Equal Terms: A Thesaurus for Nonsexist Indexing and Cataloging, 139–140
Our Bodies, Ourselves, 75
Out of the Vortex, 72–75

Photocopier, *See* copy machine
Piepmeier, Alison, x, xii, 67–71, 76, 118
Posthumus-van der Goot, Willemihn, 37–38, 40
Prejudices and Antipathies: A Tract on the LC Subject Heads Concerning People, 136–137

Punk, 66, 74, 90, 100, 110–115, 121, 125–126, 132–133, 145, 159

Queer Nation, 100
Queer Zine Archiving Project (QZAP), 162n10

Radical cataloging, 22, 123–153
Radical Reference, 123–125, 133
Radway, Janice, x, xii, 18, 79
Revolution Grrrl Style Now, vii, 86
Riot Grrrl: viii, ix, xi, 4, 15, 16, 21, 22, 53, 63–69, 71–76, 85–121, 129, 130, 133, 143–146, 148, 156, 159, 162n10, 164n41, 170n6, 172n37, 172n38, 173n63, 173n66, 174n84; collection, xi, 4, 22, 85–121, 130, 146, 156, 159, 170n8, 171n22, 172n37; manifesto, 93
Riot Grrrlz Outer Space, 59, 61

Sallie Bingham Center, 4, 14–15, 21, 55–84, 130, 167n7
Sarah Dyer Zine Collection, 57, 59, 63–67
Sarah Wood Zine Collection, 66
Schwimmer, Rosika, 33, 34, 36, 37, 39, 42, 54, 166n46
Self-publishing, 1, 14, 15, 66, 67, 129, 130, 144, 146, 169n37
Slut Magnet, 80–84
Smith College, 65
Snitow, Ann, xi, 58, 60
Steedman, Carolyn, 5
Stoler, Ann, 5, 161n6
Subcultures, 22, 88, 93, 102, 111–112, 114, 121

Taylor, Diana, 19
Taylor, Marvin, 96–97, 101
Transgender, 49, 66, 132, 141, 148, 149
Travis, Trysh, 12

Underground literature, 138. *See also* zine

Watermelon Woman, 19
Why Stories Matter, 55, 78

Women in Print, 11–12, 14
Women's Collections: Libraries, Archives and Consciousness, 32, 44
Women's Studies, 13, 26, 34, 129, 167n7, 173n66
Wooten, Kelly, xii, 2, 21, 63, 65–67, 70–71, 76
World Center for Women's Archives (WCWA), 32–44, 49
WorldCat, 128–133, 144–145, 152, 162n10

Zine, vii, viii, ix, x, xi, 1, 4, 14, 15, 16, 21–22, 55–84, 91, 92, 93, 94, 98, 105, 106, 110, 111, 112, 116, 117, 118, 123–153, 155, 156, 159, 160, 162n10, 164n41, 165n12, 167n6, 168n18, 170n6, 172n38, 174n84; collections, 4, 14, 21, 22, 55–84, 94, 98, 123–153; librarianship, 123, 132, 133, 168n18
Zine Archive and Publishing Project (ZAPP), 65, 168n18

About the Author

Kate Eichhorn is Assistant Professor of Culture and Media Studies at The New School.